Hell's Kitchen Tulagi 1942–1943

to
Gorden W. Morgan
1st Marines
Best Wishes
from
Tom "Swede" Larson

Hell's Kitchen Tulagi
1942–1943

THOMAS J. LARSON

iUniverse, Inc.
New York Lincoln Shanghai

Hell's Kitchen Tulagi 1942–1943

All Rights Reserved © 2003 by Thomas J. Larson

No part of this book may be reproduced or transmitted in any form or by any means, graphic, electronic, or mechanical, including photocopying, recording, taping, or by any information storage retrieval system, without the written permission of the publisher.

iUniverse, Inc.

For information address:
iUniverse, Inc.
2021 Pine Lake Road, Suite 100
Lincoln, NE 68512
www.iuniverse.com

Cover Design by Mary Williams Hyde

ISBN: 0-595-27756-X

Printed in the United States of America

DEDICATED TO

My two great war buddies and life long
friends Bill Rom and Ed Fearon.

Contents

Foreword. ix
Introduction xi
Preface xiii
Acknowledgements xxi
Introduction 1
CHAPTER 1   Chosen for Guadalcanal 9
CHAPTER 2   From Paradise to Hell's Kitchen 12
CHAPTER 3   The Geography of Guadalcanal, Savo, Florida And Tulagi 22
CHAPTER 4   A Brief History of Guadalcanal, Florida, Savo, And Tulagi Islands 29
CHAPTER 5   The Battle for Tulagi, Gavutu, And Tanambogo. . . . 34
CHAPTER 6   For Me the Real War Begins 38
CHAPTER 7   A Letter Home And Dengue Fever 54
CHAPTER 8   A Beachcomber on the Isle of Tulagi 64
CHAPTER 9   The Glorious Year of 1943 Starts Off With A Bang 68
CHAPTER 10   Life on Tulagi as the War Goes on 75
CHAPTER 11   The War Drags on. 82
CHAPTER 12   The War Heats up at Tulagi 92

Chapter 13	Sea Shells And Letters Home	103
Chapter 14	More Letters Home and Souvenirs	112
Chapter 15	Out of Hells Kitchen at Last!!!!!	118
Epilogue		141
Epilogue for Thomas J. Larson		149

Foreword

While showering at the Navy Northwestern University Midshipman's School in 1941, I overheard a fellow sailor talking about the famous ecologist Sigurd Olson. Being a protégé of Sig's and a student under him when he was Dean of the Ely, Minnesota Junior College, I immediately went over to meet this fellow. He turned out to be Tom Larson who had traveled over North Africa and Eastern Europe extensively in 1939 and had been lecturing at the various colleges on his travel experiences, staying with the Olson's while in Ely. We spent three months at the Navy school together and cemented a solid friendship that lasts to this day.

After graduation we all separated, I being stationed in Seattle in naval intelligence and Tom being assigned to a YP boat, eventually arriving at Pearl Harbor on December 5, 1941, two days before the big blitz. I subsequently was transferred to the battleship U.S.S. Maryland on which I served for a year, and then spent some time on Guadalcanal in naval operations. On March 7, 1943 I was transferred to the island of Tulagi and was told to unpack my sea bag in Tent No. 16. As I opened the tent flap, there on a cot sat my good friend Tom! So we had seven great months together exploring the surrounding jungle and visiting the P.T. base where John F. Kennedy was stationed, for torpedo juice, which we mixed with pineapple juice to make a potent drink. Tom had acquired the moniker the "Horrible Swede". A third mutual friend was Ed Fearon, nicknamed "Fearless Fearon" who, like Tom and me, were not particularly devoted to Navy regs as dictated by an extremely disciplined executive officer continually lording it over us.

After the war Ed built two lovely hotels on Bora Bora and Tahiti. While visiting Ed at his Tahiti Tahara Hotel after the war, a banging on the door to our room turned out to be the Horrible Swede again. Ed had assigned us a suite that was supposed to be for a Mrs. Daniels (Margaret Truman). So we had a great reunion together, reminiscing on the days of Tulagi.

To skip back, when my wife and I were married in San Francisco in 1944,. the Big Swede was stationed in nearby Livermore, and of course had to be our best man. Fearless Fearon was also stationed here and served as usher at the wedding. It was Tulagi all over again. Enroute from the Fairmont Hotel to Grace Cathedral where we were married, Tom and Ed detoured me to the Top of the Mark Hotel bar, and my future father-in-law had to rescue me so the wedding could proceed!

Tulagi was truly a devils island with its dengue and malaria fevers and extreme heat. Washing Machine Charley constantly molested us, along with a couple of good sized Jap air raids. One sank a New Zealand Corvette, the Tanker Kanahwa, and destroyer Aaron Ward during a raid of 95 Jap planes on the island. Tom and I visited one Jap bomber that had crashed behind the P.T. base and Tom recovered the tail wheel as a souvenir. When the Kanahwa was hit, survivors were being landed at the main dock where I was stationed, with burnt skin hanging down their arms. Another time Tom and I watched a series of dogfights over Lunga Point from the roof of the Governor's mansion, when 120 Jap planes hit the area in June, 1943. A PBY hit a reef at night in the harbor and I was assigned to pick up several of the bodies as they came to the surface. Our port director drowned off our dock, upon returning from a visit to a merchant marine ship where liquor was available. He apparently had one too many and missed the dock when he stepped off the tug returning him to the base.

Tom distinguished himself after the war by attaining four advanced degrees, including a doctorate in anthropology. And now he is further distinguishing himself by writing prolifically about his African and war time experiences. It is indeed a pleasure to know this great guy.

Enjoy this portion of history of WW II on the forlorn island of Tulagi.

"Wild Bill Rom"

Introduction

It is now 59 years since I left Tulagi in November of 1943. Since that time so long ago I have read many books about the bloody campaign of Guadalcanal and Tulagi. It was the first great land battle after the initial surprise successes of the Japanese after the Battle of Pearl Harbor. The myth of Japanese military superiority came to an end on Guadalcanal.

My story of my life on Tulagi during the war is taken from my journal. It tells of a viewpoint from my day-to-day life on Tulagi which began on December lst, 1942. My Guardian Spirit and fate had spared me from death of so many of my fellow Americans during the fierce struggle for possession of Guadalcanal and Tulagi during those grim days.

While Tulagi certainly deserved the name of Hells Kitchen, the nearby Florida islands were a nature-lovers escape. I had grown up in the lakes and forests country of northern Minnesota, and had an academic background in natural sciences. Lucky frequent visits to the Florida islands became a most welcome relief from the stress of heat and constant battle air raids we had on Tulagi.

Visits to fascinating Melanesian villages on the Florida islands and glimpses into their culture certainly influenced my future career as an anthropologist. Thanks also to the generous G.I. Bill that made it possible for me to return to the University of California at Berkeley to earn a BA degree in anthropology.

In 1992 1 had the delightful opportunity to live and study in a Melanesian community in New Caledonia. My main anthropological field studies were to be made in Botswana and Togo of Africa after I had earned advanced degrees at the University of Oxford and the University of Virginia.

It was unfortunate that I had been given orders to serve as liaison officer an the British cruiser HMNZS Leander damaged in a battle up in the Solomons. Coming out of Tulagi after eleven months of battle weary duty, I was not mentally prepared or properly indoctrinated to adapt to the rules and regulations and caste-like privileges of an officer in the British Navy. However, God bless her—a lovely New Zealand lady more than compensated for my unfortunate treatment on the New Zealand cruiser. And what a happy relief it was in early 1944 to be back in the United States Navy.

By war's end I had heard that about 95% of the Navy officers were citizen reserves (USNR). We of the USNR did not have a very high regard for the average Naval Academy officer with their overly exalted opinion of themselves. However I had been privileged to have served on the staffs of CinCPac and ComSoPac where I met some of the very best Naval Academy officers. I had the highest regard for Admiral Nimitz, Admiral Ghormley, and Admiral Callaghan and a few others of outstanding character who were grateful for the lowly reserves.

After all the bygone years since the war and a mellowing of memory I can honestly say that I am grateful that I had the opportunity to serve my country in World War II to help save the world for democracy.

Preface

On November 30th, 1942, it wasn't my idea of being transferred up to Guadalcanal. I was quite happy with my duty at Noumea on New Caledonia. There I was serving as a lowly Naval Reserve Ensign as a communicator on the staff of ComSoPac (Commander-in-Chief South Pacific). New Caledonia was a beautiful French colony. It was a staging base and had a large harbor for Allied ships, and training grounds for all of 252,000 of our Army and Marine Corps troops preparing to invade the long chain of islands of the Solomons to the north.

I had soon, upon my arrival at New Caledonia in July of 1942, learned to love this South Sea Island paradise. I would return to New Caledonia in 1992 to look for friends I knew in 1942, and to see more of the island I was unable to visit during the war. That story will appear in a book already written but not yet published entitled: NEW CALEDONIA AND LIFOU ISLANDS 1942–1992.

On the days when I had liberty to go ashore from the staff ship USS Argonne, I would often visit the Albie Hagen family. Mr. and Mrs. Hagen treated me as though I was one of their own sons. And yes, I even had a French girl friend, a Mademoiselle Poulette Baumier from one of the more respected families of Noumea. It was Mrs. Hagen who had so graciously introduced me to Poulette.

As a communicator my duties were mainly the encoding and decoding of messages on an electric coding machine, and delivering messages as a plugger to members of the ComSoPac staff and to ships out in the vast harbor. In this way I met the hard-pressed Admiral Ghormley of ComSoPac and his chief of Staff Admiral Daniel J. Callaghan. Admiral Callaghan and his staff were reassigned to the USS San Francisco. In the dreadful Battle of Guadalcanal on November 13th, they were all killed. I had known all these great officers while they served on ComSoPac Staff and delivered messages to them many times.

On October 18th, 1942, Admiral Nimitz and some of his CinCPac Staff visited the USS Argonne to relieve Admiral Ghormley of duty as Commander of ComSoPac and replace him with Admiral Halsey and his staff. At the staff meeting I delivered messages. There, much to my surprise, Admiral Nimitz greeted me most cordially. Back at Pearl Harbor I had delivered many messages to this great Admiral. He had always been most friendly and kind to me when I came into his office with messages.

Fate had it that I was to arrive at Pearl Harbor on December 5th, 1941. I had been the Executive officer on YP 109 (Yacht Patrol) on a stormy Pacific crossing from Long Beach, California to the Section Base In Pearl Harbor. CinCPac was in need of junior officers to train and serve as communicators. Much to my surprise I was assigned to the staff for communication training and duty.

During the four glorious months of duty with ComSoPac at Noumea I had taken to the hills all around Noumea. I would travel as far as my limited liberty hours permitted. My closest Navy buddies were Ensign Ed Fearon and Ensign Edgar Shannon. Shannon was a lucky survivor of the ill-fated heavy cruiser USS Quincy sunk at the Battle of Savo Island on August 9th, 1942. This battle had been the US Navy's worst defeat in WW II. Edgar was a loyal friend who years later became President of the University of Virginia. He had recommended me to study for my PhD in Anthropology at his university. Great friend and fellow "Free Spirit" Ed Fearon would be with me for duty up in the Solomons.

Of all the young Naval communicators on ComSoPac staff, I had served the longest in Noumea. But because of my flamboyant happy-go-lucky behavior and philosophy of life, I had been selected along with my great comrade Ed Fearon for duty at Guadalcanal, the dreaded "Island of death."

On November 30th, 1942, Ed and I and Morris Baldwin were flown up to Henderson Field on Guadalcanal. Volunteers were requested to serve in communications over on Tulagi, the Naval Base twenty miles to the north across Iron Bottom Sound. Ed, Morris Baldwin, and I quickly volunteered for this duty. I had quickly gotten the idea that Guadalcanal was not a good place for my philosophy of life. And, it was on December 1st, 1942, we arrived on Tulagi the day of a night sea battle out on Iron Bottom Sound. And on that date my story about Hell's Kitchen Tulagi really begins as taken from my forbidden diary.

The word got out on Tulagi that we were not permitted to keep diaries as it was feared that they might possibly fall into enemy hands and give them useful information. However, ever since I was eleven years old I had written diaries. I was not about to quit now. What good fortune! On the floor of the badly bombed British Colonial Residence were scattered copies of official correspondence paper. I eagerly gathered them up and would use them for recording my Tulagi story. Also I got around the regulation by writing letters to sisters and my parents which were never sent. My off-and-on recording of the events of my life on Tulagi I chose to name: HELL'S KITCHEN TULAGI (1942–1943).

For eleven months I served on Tulagi until fatigue, fever, jungle rot, had me staggering around like a zombie. I became what was known in the Solomons as "Rock Happy" While my buddy Ed Fearon got sent States Side on an American ship, I had the sad fate and misfortune to be reassigned to the HMNZS Leander. This was a British New Zealand light cruise whose bow had been hit by a Jap torpedo in the Battle of Kolombangaro. She was to sail from Auckland to Boston Naval Yard for repairs.

War weary and staggering around in a daze in the sweltering heat off Tulagi my new assignment should never have been given to me. I was never given any orientation as to how to serve as a liaison officer on a caste-ridden British ship with all their officer privileges and regulations. How was I who had mingled freely with my enlisted men, and living in mud, heavy rain, and taking refuge under coconut logs during air raids, possibly know how to fit into the officer caste system of a British war ship? I was headed for trouble soon after I set foot on the deck of the Leander.

Well! Back-tracking I state: What was my life like while I served on Tulagi? Though there many scary days from frequent Jap air raids, and night bombings from Washing Machine Charlie, I managed to have some happy experiences. I developed great friendships with Ed "Dreamer" Fearon, and "Wild" Bill Rom. There was also great buddy Morris Baldwin, and many of the young officers assigned for duty in communications,. I became good friends with many of my great radio gang, the survivors from the aircraft carrier Hornet, lost in a great battle in the Eastern Solomons. While I was in charge of the radio station, I managed to get most of my deserving radiomen promoted before the Executive Officer, Commander Jones, realized what I was doing.

With Ed Fearon and Bill Rom, we made numerous trips exploring war ravaged Tulagi, the nearby islands, and visits to the PT Base along the Hutchinson Creek over on Florida Island. There we survived very potent Torpedo juice cocktails, and looked for souvenirs of parts of downed Jap planes in the nearby jungle. I made expeditions with General Fuller and some of his Army officers way up along Florida to Olivuga Island. Whenever I got some liberty, I would go to Halavo over on Florida Island to barter for fruit and souvenirs in native villages. On one grand liberty day I was over to Guadalcanal to look for souvenirs on the battlefields. An Army officer drove me in his Jeep to the Matanikau River to the scene of a great battle. There I came upon dead Japs not yet buried. A Japanese soldier contributed his rifle and helmet to me which I still have in my den. Thank you sir. I wish you happy days in your Shinto Heaven.

Once back in the US at Boston Naval Yard, I happily became liberated from the cruel caste-ridden Leander. At Com One, while requesting duty back in the good old American Navy, I met the gorgeous Navy Wave officer Ensign Agnes Gilbert, a Powers model from Kentucky. She befriended me.

At the first opportunity I took a train down to Washington D.C., and to the Naval Personnel office. There a kind Navy Commander, who was a survivor of the ill-fated USS Quincy in the Battle of Savo Island, told me since I had been so long out in the war zone I could have any duty I wished. I asked him, "Where In California is a base with the best food?" He replied, "Naval Air Station Livermore." The orders were written and I had a month's leave. I served for over a year at this great Navy Primary Flight Training Base, then feeling it was my duty to get back into the fighting Navy, I requested sea duty. I was assigned to the repaired aircraft carrier USS Lexington. As a deck officer with duty on the bridge we cruised off the coast of Japan in the biggest combined American and British fleets the world had ever seen. I felt the concussion of the two atom bombs 200 miles out at sea. Then Hurrah! The war was over! We had won! For two days I had the most interesting liberty in Yokosuka Naval Base in Tokyo Bay.

THE EVOLUTION TO A SAILOR

Top Left: Professor Tom "Okavango" Larson——1919. At age two giving a speech at Mora, Minnesota in 1919. Top right: A brand new 12-year-old Boy Scout of Aitkin, Minnesota. 1929.
Bottom left: In 1934 at age 17 Tom Larson is a National Guardsman of Co.B 135 Minnesota Infantry.
Bottom right: From a Buck private to a Lt. Comdr. USNR, in Yokasuka, Tokyo Bay, 1945.

Naval Reserve Midshipman Thomas J. Larson at Panama City, Panama, in August 1940 on his training cruise. During the summer of 1941 he would take his three months training at Northwestern University at the Chicago campus, then when commissioned Ensign, be on active duty. He was sent to San Diego for training in Naval Intelligence.

Preface   xix

We are the "Honorable" Ninety Day wonders, class of summer of 1941-DVGs from Tower Hall of the downtown campus of Northwestern University of Chicago. Of 1200 cadets taken from many universities all over the United States, 600 would graduate. Some would die in the war, some would command ships, all of us would have great adventures serving our country and saving the world from the tyranny of Japan and Hitler.

Many would go on after the war to distinguished careers in many honorable fields of endeavor. One of my classmates here died when the Cruiser Juneau was sunk. Tom Fernading was wounded and saved when the heavy cruiser was sunk during the August 9th, 1942, battle off Savo Island.

Acknowledgements

War is terrible! Yet there are-some good things which come out of war. First of all World War II saved the civilized world for democracy, and stopped the horrible and evil deeds of Hitler's Nazis and the cruel and sadistic Japanese bent upon world conquest. For America it got the country out of the great depression of the thirties. It created employment for all who wished for it-yes everyone who was not already in a military uniform. For those in our military and in combat areas, it offered them friendship with their fellow comrades, and the peoples in the lands where they helped liberate and occupy. For most of our troops who had never ventured far from home, it gave them the great opportunity to travel. This was a profound experience as American service personnel became scattered far and wide over the world. These American men and women would never be the same.

The best thing that World War II did for me was to give me two life-long friends—Bill Rom and Ed Fearon—who served with me on Tulagi. Many other war time friends I remember but unfortunately had lost contact with them. They will be mentioned as my story unfolds.

I thank the generous U.S. Navy for giving me adventure, travel, good pay, and promotions. On New Caledonia I am most grateful to the generous members of the Albie Hagen family. I thank Poulette Beamier of Noumea for her friendship. Enroute to Guadalcanal Ed Fearon and I met the adorable Ramon and Loulette Hill sisters in Thio, New Caledonia. These lovely young women gave us much hospitality in their South Sea Island Paradise.

In Auckland New Zealand in early November of 1943, I thank the lovely Miss Doris Mears for her kindness in taking care of my needs. On Tulagi FATE it was that I had the good fortune with Ed Fearon, Bill Rom, and Morris Baldwin to be ordered to move up to the old British Colonial residence which had been partially bombed when the Marines and U.S. Navy invaded the island. I thank the great members of my radio gang-the survivors of the U.S.S. Hornet aircraft carrier.

We all appreciated our Marine messenger Hatfield of the infamous clan of Hatfields of West Virginia. This talented young man provided us with his fantastic home brew for keeping up our morale.

Ed, Bill and I made frequent visits to the PT Base along Hutchinson Creek over on Florida Island. There we searched for souvenirs up in the jungle from downed Jap planes. And, we survived potent torpedo juice cocktails. I thank the Navy for granting me liberty for taking small boat trips up along the Florida Island coast to fascinating native villages. I met Chief Patrick over at a native village on Halavo where he offered me a native wife for twenty tins of corn beef. I could never gather together that much corn beef for the bride wealth required.

We of the radio gang were most grateful to, the 26th CBies for blasting a cave for our radio operations. Previously we had to close down operations and head for a fox hole every time we had a Jap air raid. I am especially grateful for a glorious liberty over on Guadalcanal so I could search for souvenirs. A kind Army officer drove me up to a recent battlefield along the Matanikau River. Thank a poor unfortunate Japanese soldier who was killed in this battle and now gave me the honor of taking care of his rifle and helmet.

I had a very special native Melanesian scout friend, Constable S. M. Salana of Auki, Malaita. This kind friend gave me a wonderful mahogany war club and other souvenirs. We corresponded for several years. He had collected many Japanese scalps on his patrols in the jungle at Guadalcanal and Florida Island.

Besides the many malaria infected great radio gang friends, I especially remember Kid Conner of the Main Line of Philadelphia, Kellogg, Bavis, Dick Hill, Tom Stoddard who was the only one on Tulagi who could repair the electric coding machines. There was that old tattooed and crusty Australian planter Harper who befriended us and told us many wild stories of his life in the islands.

My book would not be complete without a Tulagi villain. This honor went to the mean-spirited Executive officer Commander J. In comparison Captain O.O. Kessing (known as OOK the omnipotent) was our base commander. Considering his Annapolis education, he was a pretty good man to compensate for "Sad Sack" J.

When I finally got back to America to Com One at Boston, I thank God for getting me off that HMNZS British cruiser Leander which was caste-ridden with so many snobbish officers who gave me a bad time. However their enlisted seamen and petty officers were fine friendly New Zealanders. Good fortune soon came to me at Com One when the gorgeous Ensign Agnes Gilbert of Kentucky and an ex Powers model took command of me and gave me great kindness and friendship. Down in Washington D.C. I headed for Navy Personnel to get back into the American Navy. A kind commander, who had been a lucky survivor of the ill-fated heavy CRUISER QUINCY sunk in the Battle of Savo island, came to my rescue. God bless him. He gave me orders to report to Naval Air Station Livermore in California where I had duty for over a year.

I thank all the many young American girls I corresponded with during my stay on Tulagi. These patriotic young ladies and my sisters and parents all wrote to me to help keep up my morale. And yes, it was God who saved me from a bout of Dengue Fever. All in all the eleven months on Tulagi was quite an experience.

Last of all, I am grateful to my brother-in-law Ben Kerns who introduced me to Mary Williams Hyde. This highly skilled woman scans my books and gets them to my publisher, Writers Club Press of Lincoln, Nebraska.

Introduction

In 1937 as an Eagle Rover scout I'd set out from my home town of Aitkin, Minnesota, with a packsack on my back. I would see the world and be an ambassador of good will. Eighteen months later I escaped out of Europe four months before Hitler's legions thundered into Poland and began World War Two. Fate it was and destiny was to most dramatically initiate me into the United States Navy and into World War Two. So now my story can begin.

REMEMBER PEARL HARBOR!

Day after day that first week of December 1941, the U.S. Navy's puny patrol yacht from California struggled through heavy seas and rough weather, slip-sliding her way to Pearl Harbor—and a day of destiny.

First person by Thomas J. Larson

As a young naval reserve ensign I'd always heard it said that the U.S. Navy liked to enlist men from the farms and small towns of the Midwest. The Navy brass welcomed men who were familiar with hard work.

My home town of Aitkin, Minnesota, qualified all right. It was a small farming community 130 miles north of Minneapolis in the woods along the Mississippi River.

And whoever heard of a place called Pearl Harbor?

After my second year at the University of Minnesota in 1937, I'd started a vagabond journey around the world as part of my education as a Rover Boy Scout. Four months before Nazi Germany invaded Poland in 1939, I took warning and was able to work passage home from Europe.

When I saw Minnesota again, I had worked as a seaman on the Pat Doheny, a California tanker, the Robert Maersk, a Danish freighter, and the Nordfjord, a Norwegian freighter. Although I was what the Annapolis officers termed a "ninety-day wonder" and a "feather merchant, with an old Viking name like Larson I took to the sea the moment I first set foot on deck. By August of 1940 I'd taken a Naval Reserve cruise on the battleship New York to Panama, and Guantanamo Bay in Cuba. I then became a midshipman in the V-7 program at Northwestern University in Chicago. Commissioned as a reserve ensign on September 13, 1941. I had orders to report to the naval pier at San Diego for training in naval intelligence. After three weeks there, I was assigned to the destroyer base as a junior security officer.

Then, in the middle of some interesting duty and training, I received new and unexpected orders. I was to be the executive officer (there were only two officers) on Yacht Patrol (YP) 109. This boat was to be sailed to Pearl Harbor, from which point it would patrol the Hawaiian Islands. When YP 109 had been delivered to the section base at Pearl, I was to return to the destroyer base in San Diego. All very simple and forthright. California to Pearl, Pearl to California.

On November 10, I reported to the naval director's office at San Pedro. There I had my first look at the beautiful 115-foot pleasure yacht, the Elvida, previously owned by a millionaire lawyer from Los Angeles. The reserve ensign in command was from Hollywood and had been in the NAVY several months longer than I. We had 15 men on board and a small half grown kitten named Tiger.

On November 12, we made trial runs. We spent a whole day, November 24, 1941, getting last minute supplies aboard. After taking on oil in the afternoon, we slepped back to the repair base. The next day we would steam for Pearl Harbor.

The countdown had begun, only we didn't know it.

On Tuesday, November 25, we cast off our lines at 0730. We steamed out beyond the breakwater. We then had to standby for the ship we were to accompany, the tanker Ramapo.

At 0900, the Ramapo came out beyond the breakwater. We took position 1000 yards off her port stern.

Soon we were nearing Santa Catalina Island. I enjoyed a wonderful dinner. Our cook, a seaman named Schraeder from West Virginia (I don't recall all the first names) was very proficient. Tiger, the kitten entertained us by chasing walnuts and scampering around on deck.

I went on watch with Seaman 1st class Warren in the wheelhouse. We communicated by radio with the Ramapo every hour. Sea birds, seals and porpoises were in great numbers. After passing Santa Barbara Island, a barren mountain peak, we approached San Clemente Island on our port side.

I saw clouds to the west, but the weather was still fair.

Next day, the 26th, I took the midnight watch with coxswain Houghton from Aberdeen S.D. We followed the tanker, just in sight of her wake light. The barometer still read fair weather, though the sky was now overcast.

None of us knew, of course, that on November 26, a task force of six carriers set sail from home port in Japan—and promptly disappeared from Western eyes.

The following day, the 27th, I took the 0800 morning watch and saw the sea picking up. In fact, the weather was rapidly getting worse. By suppertime there were only six of us who were not seasick. Tiger was as lively as ever.

In the morning we had a man-overboard drill. It rained a little, the barometer fell to 30. The seas had picked up considerably. A real storm lay ahead.

Friday the 28th dawned, and we lost sight of the Ramapo for a while in the night. Fortunately, the old tanker came into view again. So many of our men were down with seasickness that I had to stand a watch all night long.

All the furniture had to be lashed down. From my journal: "The boat labors, creaks, and groans. We bank into heavy seas on and on. The barometer is still falling."

Thoughts of sanctuary at Pearl.

In the afternoon, when I was trying to catch a few winks, the Ramapo nearly hit us. Although we were supposed to be following her, we would get ahead of her with our faster engines.

Later we received a message from the Ramapo to darken ship as there was danger of enemy submarines around Hawaiian waters.

No war, but darken ship?

On Saturday, November 29, the sun actually came out for a while. Everyone who could eat had to prepare his own food, since even the cook hadn't been on his feet for two days. We couldn't sleep below decks because fumes from the engine room poisoned the air. Most of the men tried to sleep in the wardroom.

People prayed for us to hurry up and get to Pearl Harbor!

The rough weather and seas picked up again. No hot food still. The cook stayed in his bunk. I was surprised that some of the older seamen got so seasick.

I couldn't sleep. The wind blew the gas from the galley right back on us. With no good air below, we felt suffocated and got bursting headaches.

November 30 was a Sunday. The last Sunday before December began.

Journal talk again. "December 1st, Monday—Tiger the kitten, was up in the wheelhouse chasing raindrops. He kept us all laughing and prevented us from getting on each other's nerves. For a short while the sun came out. Everyone came out of hibernation and looked a little more cheerful. The cook actually got us some warm food. However, we still couldn't eat off the table—nothing would stay on it.

All afternoon the boys played poker while I read and tried to sleep. I even had the rare luxury of a hot bath. And then, a wild beautiful night! Huge long swells rolled across, coming down from the north. We wallowed along in the trough of the great waves.

On December 2, the weather was fine, much warmer and we had sunshine. The seas had calmed down considerably.

One of our engines went out of commission for awhile as the Ramapo stood by. They sent us over some bread, apples, cabbages, and potatoes. All during this operation the kitten was pouncing around on deck, putting on a hilarious exhibition to the amusement of everyone.

Finally we got our engine repaired and got underway. Only three more days to Pearl!

Wednesday, the 3rd, found the wind with us, high waves drove us rapidly along toward Hawaii. We had regular meals—cook was on his feet again!

Journal talk: "December 4th, Thursday—The seas and the wind still with us as we rolled along like a surfboard. I got some of the salt out of my shoes by rubbing them with a raw potato. Time passed rapidly. The men were more cheerful now. Just about everyone eating again."

December 5, Friday—When I awakened, I peered out of the porthole and saw one of the Hawaiian islands. I was told it was Molokai. It had high hills and was rather barren but still inviting. The blue sea and sky were enthralling as we merrily raced along toward destiny.

In the early afternoon we saw Diamond Head as we approached Honolulu and Pearl Harbor.

We followed the Ramapo into Pearl Harbor and tied up at the section base just inside the breakwater. The fleet was in. I counted the great battleships.

I accompanied the YP captain to the section base headquarters, where we reported to the section base commander. With that business completed, the captain headed for Honolulu on liberty. I remained on board the YP that evening.

December 6, a Saturday, dawned. In the morning I reported to the section base commander. He commended me for our bringing YP-109 in from San Pedro. Then, much to my surprise, I was handed orders to report to CINCPAC (Commander-in Chief, Pacific) staff at the submarine base for duty as a communicator. My dream of cruising the Hawaiian Islands in beautiful Yacht Patrol 109 was shattered.

At the staff communications office of CINCPAC that Saturday, I met my new boss, Lt. J.G. East, a Naval Academy graduate who was very cheerful and congenial.

I moved into the bachelor officers' quarters (BOQ), near the submarine base. This was a three-storied building surrounded by palm trees—I thought maybe shore duty might not be so bad after all. I even planned some hikes into the mountains.

That late afternoon I saw a perfect rainbow spread in a wide arc across the green mountains above Pearl Harbor. I went to bed quite early, without the slightest forewarning that the next morning's events would change the history of the world.

Journal talk again. "December 7th, Sunday Lieutenant J.G. Herb Fairchild (from Berkeley, Calif.) and I were leisurely walking toward the submarine base, where CINCPAC had its headquarters. I would report for my first duty and training at my new post. Chirping noisily, the mynah birds heralded a lovely sunny day. My sea legs were not used to solid ground. I admired the lovely tropical trees. Breathing deeply, I enjoyed the wonderful fragrance of the balmy air."

It was about 7:45 a.m.. We would relieve the night watch a bit early as was polite naval custom. While we walked along in our tropical whites, we saw low single-engine planes above us to our left.

"How interesting." I thought. "Maneuvers on Sunday."

Not far away, I heard anti-aircraft guns shooting.

Ahead of us was a large spreading tree. I waved nonchalantly up at a pilot in one of the planes. I noticed a few leaves fluttering down from the tree. At the time I didn't think anything of it. But green leaves do not just flutter down by themselves. A burst from a machine gun must have dropped them. How else? The wind wasn't blowing.

All around us men ran for shelter. More planes flew low over head—over the submarine base toward Ford Island and our battleships. Now, there were more scattered bursts of .50 caliber gunfire and antiaircraft. Overhead a plane with a red rising insignia burst into flames. It plunged into the water nearby.

As we walked around the corner of the sub base headquarters building, I saw more men running for cover, into the building. Nothing yet had dawned on me. I still thought I was witnessing American military maneuvers. "But why did they have to have them on Sunday!" was my thought.

I followed Fairchild into the building and up to the second floor, which was the headquarters for all the top officers of CINCPAC staff. How did a lowly Naval Reserve ensign like me ever become an officer of this great staff? I had to wonder.

Someone in the communication office said we were at war. Unbelievable! The Japanese were bombing us! I was in a state of shock. I remember I had no fear. Just compete surprise.

No one had any time to give me any training. Lieutenant East shoved a clipboard in my hands and said I was "officer messenger plugger." Freshly decoded messages were to be delivered by me to the various staff officers. All such messages of course were top secret and urgent.

That fateful morning I was in and out of Admiral Kimmel's office many times. He was a lean middle-aged man with a fiery temper. He wasn't at all like the actors playing his part in the later movies. Far from being very cool and collected, the real Admiral Kimmel was cursing and ranting and raving whenever he read all the dreadful messages I brought to him about battleships blowing up and sinking, the planes and hangers on Ford Island being demolished, and the Army's Schofield Barrack's being bombed and strafed.

He was red faced and completely flustered. I didn't blame him and didn't resent his anger at my many appearances with nothing but bad news. Of all the staff officers I delivered messages to that sad morning—and there were many—it was Admiral Kimmel I would remember most vividly. He had to take all the blame. The rest of his staff was kept on when Admiral Chester Nimitz arrived later to take command of CINCPAC. Kimmel was relieved.

When I wasn't delivering messages to the staff and carrying the replies back to the communication office, I was up on the roof of the sub base building watching the battle. I still had no fear. I was in a complete state of shock. As that dreadful morning went on, I saw the battleships being destroyed. the Oklahoma rolled over, the Arizona sinking, the others trying to get underway, the Nevada making it to a mud bank, and all hell exploding over on Ford Island.

Later that day our staff of ensigns was increased with survivors from the stricken battleships. One, a small man, had slipped through a porthole when the Oklahoma rolled over. He told me a broad officer behind him was too big to slip through and was left in the ship to die. Other junior officers had been rescued from the oily water. A few lucky ones had been on liberty and were ashore in Honolulu that morning.

Still without fear I went about the grim messenger duty and returned often to the roof to watch my first great naval battle. Now flames and loud explosions were all over Pearl Harbor. Our guns were shooting at the enemy planes as no longer sleepy crewmen and officers got to their battle stations. Rescue boats were pulling men out of the water who were covered with thick, burning oil, A few enemy planes were being hit by our guns and exploding into the water.

By evening back at the BOQ my shock was wearing off. At last the full realization came to me—I was in a WAR! And naturally I was restricted to base. No hikes into the mountains anytime soon. Anti-aircraft shells were still exploding and machine guns rattled. Even dogs, they say, were being shot by trigger-happy sentries. Anything that moved that night was in danger of being shot.

Rumor had it that a Japanese invasion fleet was on its way to Oahu We were hurriedly issued side arms. And during the night an anti-aircraft shell went through the ceiling and floor of the BOQ room next to mine. I was nervous, jittery, and angry at the enemy. The shock was over. I had been initiated—not only into the US Navy, but also into WAR.

In the middle of the night I heard shooting and shrapnel and machine gun bullets flying around. I was plenty scared after all that I'd seen the day before. I had a strange feeling never before experienced, a very tense feeling. The air-raid alarm was an awful scary-sounding thing. I huddled close to a corner to avoid stray bullets. Even my British roommate was uneasy, and he had been in the Battle of Dunkirk.

As I heard later, our own planes had flown overhead and were shot at by our anti-aircraft guns. Everyone was jittery and light on the trigger. I couldn't sleep very well and was uneasy all day at work. I jumped at any loud banging or rumbling noise. No one in the communication office had any time to train me in communications. So, to kill time, I went up on the roof to talk to the machine-gun crews there. The Arizona was still smoking, though most of her was under water.

More journal talk. "December 9th, Tuesday—I met many men from the ill-fated ships that were victims of the fury of the Jap attacks. They told me some bloody and terrible stories. America is furious now and is finally united and out for revenge because of the treacherous surprise attack. Germany and Italy have now declared war on us. The morale here is fine, even though several thousand of our men were killed. We aren't allowed off the base. Marine guards are super eager on the trigger, and have done a lot of shooting. Wild rumors are flying around like mad and most of them untrue. One doesn't know what to believe.

December 10th, Wednesday—We are seeing some of the battleships being repaired. The Tennessee is still hemmed in by the California, but is in good shape. We will be able to salvage and repair the Maryland, the Pennsylvania, and Nevada is still stuck in the mud bank and getting up steam to get away from Battleship Row.

The national battle cry now is 'Remember Pearl Harbor!' I will never forget that battle! Already there is a song out called 'Remember Pearl Harbor!'

Meanwhile, I was usually just getting in the way in the communications office. Once in awhile, they'd have a job for me. Every night in a different room I slept. "Am often rudely awakened by air raid threats. I dress hurriedly and rush downstairs from the third floor, where I seem to think bombs won't get me. These are all false alarms.

On December 11, during the hours off duty, I thumbed a ride over to the section base to see "my little ship"—the Elvida (YP 109). The crew had painted her and I hardly recognized her. The boys were all fine. No one had been hurt, even though a bomb had dropped nearby.

I then hitch over to Hickam Airfield, where scores of men had been killed in their barracks. "The place was in ruins." I wrote in my journal. "Many of our planes were destroyed. The place was in a terrible mess. But the Japanese will pay for their big mistake—Britain, Holland, and other countries have declared war on Japan. She will have no chance to win this war she started."

Later, after seven months with CINCPAC, I served with COMSOPAC staff for four months in New Caledonia. From there I was sent to Naval Base Tulagi for 11 months in the Solomons. I was sent back to the States as a liaison officer on the damaged light cruiser Leander a New Zealand ship. After a year at Naval Air Station Livermore in California, I finished the war on the second aircraft carrier Lexington when she steamed triumphantly into Tokyo Bay with the US Seventh Fleet.

A journal entry on December 11, four days after Pearl Harbor had been correct. "Japan," it said, "had started the war, but Japan could not win the war."

1

Chosen for Guadalcanal

It was on September 15th, 2000 when I sat down to begin to tell my story. I had been thinking about writing a book for some time. My story about my war time duty on Tulagi twenty miles across Iron Bottom Sound from Guadalcanal is taken mostly from my notes and copies of letters I'd written on Solomon Island Administration paper. From the partially bombed out residence, I had fortunately found this paper scattered on the floor asking to be rescued. The keeping of diaries was forbidden by the Navy because it was feared that useful information might fall into Japanese hands. There was also fear that the enemy might attempt a landing on Tulagi which fortunately never did occur. The land fighting was still raging over on Guadalcanal. Tulagi had almost daily attacks by aircraft during the time of my duty there beginning on November 30th, 1942, and ending in November of 1943.

The savage fighting of the First Marine Division and Raider Battalion in the taking of Tulagi and nearby islands has been described in many books about the battle for Guadalcanal. I will describe it briefly as I was to live amidst the devastation of our naval and aircraft bombardment prior to our invasion by the Marines. My story will be mostly about the daily life with the members of my radiomen who were the survivors of the aircraft carrier Hornet in the Battle of Santa Cruz Islands, and with my fellow young communicator officers.

I'd already written an as yet unpublished book about my Naval experiences in World War II entitled NEW CALEDONIA-1942. My entry into combat in World War II came suddenly on December 7th, 1941, when only two days previously I'd arrived at the Section Base in Pearl Harbor as an Ensign Executive officer on Y P. 109 (Yacht Patrol) after a stormy crossing of the Pacific out of Long Beach, California. That fateful morning I was delivering messages to Admiral Kimmel and had been assigned to communications duty on his CinCPac staff. The story leading up to my training to become a Naval Reserve officer I'd written in another as yet unpublished book I'd named: THE LOVES AND WAR FOR ENSIGN SWEDE LARSON.

The story about my assignment to go to Hell's Kitchen Tulagi I'd chosen to begin on November 26th, 1942. I'd been serving as a communication officer on the ComSoPac staff of Admiral Halsey in Noumea, New Caledonia harbor. As my story progresses, there will be numerous flashbacks such as the description of Tulagi and nearby islands and the savage struggle for their capture.

From my manuscript NEW CALEDONIA-1942, Chapter Ten, "Selected for Guadalcanal," I begin. Life was becoming more and more bearable and interesting every day. Though I never did like office jobs, this one in the sweltering humid heat of the communication office gave me the opportunity to get ashore in the fascinating French colonial town of Noumea.

On my liberty days, about every fourth day, I could ride Australian cavalry horses along the beautiful Dumbea River. I visited the Kanak villages in lush valleys with multi-colored flowers and delicious fruits. In true beachcomber fashion I would head for the many lovely beaches of Noumea and surrounding areas accompanied often by attractive young French lassies. I was most fortunate in receiving great hospitality from the Albie Hagen family who had so graciously adopted me and treated me as one of their own sons. I'd spent delightful hours ashore exploring the musty wares of the out-of-the-way shops in search of old relics, books, batik cloth, sea shells, and souvenirs.

At my work with my fellow young officers and radiomen I kept up a continuous flow of boisterous singing and conversation as I encoded and decoded urgent messages to and from the bloody fighting on Guadalcanal. I tried to forget that there was a war, and to make all those around me forget it too. How could I always be talking shop even though it was about the sinking of ships, the loss of our brave aviators, and the fierce fighting of our Marines and Army troops on the ground. It was another terrible war, and this one especially was one which had to be fought to save the civilized world. It was the greatest and the most devastating and most important war in the history of mankind and the world.

Yes, I always tried to be cheerful in spite of the gravity of our precarious toehold on Guadalcanal and the devastating sea battles around Savo Island and Iron Bottom Sound. My immediate supervisor in the communication office was a miserable, fat-bellied, soft, pale faced cranky and irritable Lt. J.G.—yes, and a reserve officer. He announced to me and everyone on our watch that I had been especially chosen to go to Guadalcanal. It was obvious that I was having too much fun. This miserable character had decided to dispose of Swede Larson from ComSoPac staff. At first he asked me to volunteer for the "Great Honor" to go to

Guadalcanal. But this time I did not volunteer as I had up at Pearl Harbor to join ComSoPac staff which was at that time down in Auckland, New Zealand with all those beautiful and most friendly young eager women.

Oh yes! Fate it was who had ordained that I should be sent to the Island of Death. Of course, after enjoying New Caledonia so much, I wasn't all that eager to be sent to Guadalcanal. But I was told that I had the very special honor of being chosen-yes, I who had been on the staff the longest while many of the other young officers on our communication staff had only recently come up from Auckland where they had the delightful opportunity to enjoy the friendship of the many young ladies of that fabulous and beautiful land. Most of the men and boys of military age in New Zealand had gone off to war where so many would die. Their women, desperate and eager for love, would meet our Navy men and Marines stationed and training there. In James Michener's book, RETURN TO PARADISE, he told the sad story of the young New Zealand women who had husbands, fathers, brothers and sons lost in the war. My turn to meet a lovely New Zealand woman would come after I'd spent my time at Tulagi-Hell's Kitchen. And yes, I will add in spite of all the misery Hell's Kitchen would give me, some of my greatest friendships I would experience there which would influence my life so profoundly. I was not the only chosen culprit selected for Guadalcanal. Ensign Ed Fearon, another carefree fellow communicator who shared my free spirit and many of my ideas and philosophy of life was also told that he-had the dubious honor for duty at Guadalcanal.

We were to be ready to leave by six the next morning. I immediately ran up to Hagen's house in Noumea, the nice home of my New Caledonia family. The rest of the day I made mad attempts to finish my packing and collecting the necessary equipment for going up to the front lines. My last supper with the Hagens and their youngest son Peter was very quiet and sad. I bade them farewell with many of my sincere thanks for their great kindness and hospitality and returned to the USS Argonne to hurriedly make my last preparations for departure. I slept on the deck of the old Argonne staff ship for the last time. Though my mind was troubled I slept peacefully.

In 1992 I made a historical return trip to New Caledonia to be one of three US WW II veterans to represent the 50th anniversary of the first American troops to arrive in Noumea in March of 1942. The elder Hagens were long gone. But, I did find their son Peter who was fourteen in 1942. He and his gracious wife welcomed me and gave me great hospitality. I also found the beautiful Andrea Baumier the young sister of my good friend Poulette who had died.

2

From Paradise to Hell's Kitchen

Early in the morning of November 27th, 1942, Ed Fearon and I were up and ready to get up to the Tontouta military airport by 9 o'clock. The chosen five of us finally got into Noumea and got transportation to the airfield 30 miles to the north. Of course no one there knew anything about our going up to Guadalcanal by plane. No sweat! This suited Ed and I just fine. We arranged for a ride in a DC-3 transport plane for the next day instead of returning to the old Argonne.

I quickly thought of a most interesting plan. Why not go over the mountains to Thio where the two beautiful Hill sisters Ramon and Loulette lived? Now was our chance for one last day of freedom before heading into a most uncertain fate. My buddy Ed I soon was able to talk into my glorious idea. Soon we were on our happy way to Thio by hitch hiking.

New Caledonia was alive with US military vehicles on the road. A common saying in New Caledonia in those war-time days "that there was a G I peeing behind every bush". In all there were 250,000 American military on the island training during the war with more Navy personnel on up to 100 ships in the great harbor at times.

We soon had a ride up to the town of Bouloupari where an army truck driver gave us a ride inland over the mountain a few miles. To get to Thio on the east side of New Caledonia we had to go over a one-way road across a mountain ridge. As traffic was coming from the opposite direction, we accepted an invitation from a generous army officer to have dinner with him at his camp. His outfit was from the eastern states and the American Division made up of different outfits. In this camp we met a huge corporal who had been an all-American football player. Our officer friend told us this was a rather stupid and lazy soldier.

After our free meal sponsored by Uncle Sam, Ed and I lay in the shade of a great tree until we heard the loud noise of two army Jeeps approaching which aroused us into action. Hailing the drivers for a ride, we met four parachutists Raider Battalion Marines who were heading for Thio. These fellows had just come up from Auckland New Zealand where they had recovered from wounds from fighting at Tulagi and Guadalcanal. Now they were enjoying a much deserved leave before being sent into more combat.

Our driver followed the steep one-way road up through the jungle and over the summit where we had the first view of the east side of the 230 mile long island. A beautiful blanket of different shades of green spread out before us which was broken only by outcroppings of reddish earth from nickel mines. Our Marine driver took our breath away as he made hairpin turns at reckless speed in a Jeep that appeared to have no brakes. Any moment of this exciting ride at every sharp curve in the road we expected to crash head on to an on-coming vehicle. Three times we met army trucks but luckily found wide places in the road. We could look down over hundreds of feet of shear rock cliffs to the forest and a river below. One of our Marine friends was a clean-cut fellow named Jacobson-a Swede from Minneapolis, Minnesota-my home state. He told us that he had lost all of his enthusiasm as a parachutist. He had made a parachute landing behind Jap lines on Guadalcanal and luckily made it back wounded to his Raider outfit.

Soon our valley broadened out; the river became larger and deeper and the land more fertile. Small farms appeared, cattle, and a few inhabitants came into view. At the mouth of a beautiful river we came upon the little village of Thio with its Catholic church and Mission station. Never before had I seen such a quiet, peaceful, and picturesque village.

Soon we were plunging into the cool water of the river. Then we visited the Catholic cathedral with its Mission surrounded by a native Kanak village. Though the individual houses of the village were untidy and not clean, the streets beautiful and laid out in perfect order. Half naked black little Melanesian natives clustered around us to have their pictures taken.

As we were unable to buy any fruit from the natives, we returned to Thio. A colonial law had just been passed forbidding any New Caledonian to sell locally grown fruit and vegetables to the Americans. The poor people were almost unable to get necessary food supplies to live on. Every ship, on the other hand, brought food supplies to American occupying troops.

To our surprise we learned that not any American troops were stationed here. Also we learned to our delight that there were about 25 eligible young unmarried girls in Thio. I knew that two lovely young girls—Ramon and Loulette Hill lived here. We had been introduced to them when they had recently visited Andrea and Poulette Baumier in Noumea. Luckily we now found them at home, and were welcomed heartily. The sisters were glad to see us as they were bored with the quiet life in Thio.

Beautiful sexy Ramon was an adorable flirt who drove us love starved GI's to distraction and desire for her. Most of the local French colonial girls had great sex appeal. And Ramon had far more than her share of this desirable quality. She spoke English like a New Zealander. Though she lacked the healthy American corn-fed look of girls from my home state of Minnesota and Iowa farm raised products, they were here and that was the most important thing to our troops. Ramon's well-shaped bare legs, a slim waist, and well-formed breasts under a loose-fitting blouse drove me to instant distraction.

Loulette was a few years older than Ramon, about twenty, and had most of the attractive characteristics of her sister Ramon. From a recent appendicitis operation Loulette was still a little palled and under the weather. The outnumbered ladies now invited a young French schoolteacher to join us. This Andrea was a dark-haired and healthy looking girl with sparkling laughing brown eyes and big dimples.

Our young Marine Raider parachutist driver Jacobson drove us all out into the country with the girls to get some fresh pineapples from a farmer. Then in the cool of the valley country road, the sun was setting. Its fading rays spread down across the red hills above. Soon deep purple shadows enveloped us. I thought how could all this be true. Here we were in a heavenly paradise with these God's divine feminine creatures. Soon we would be sent to dreaded Guadalcanal, the Island of Death. No moment in our Paradise must be wasted for tomorrow we would be flown into a different world where there were no Ramons, Loulettes, and Andreas.

Now the high-spirited and delightful young women invited us to dinner in the Hill's simple cottage. Though citizens of New Caledonia, the sisters had a Scots father and a local French mother. We met the father, a small dried-up jovial character. At one time he had been a notorious alcoholic as well as the best dentist of the island. He had left Noumea to bring his beautiful daughters to remote Thio where they wouldn't be constantly molested by soldiers and sailors.

The golden moon was full with its majestic splendor spreading across the valley as Jacobson drove us with the three girls out into the country to the riverbank. We spread out a canvas under the glory of the Heavens, then feasted on the sweet pineapples. We were serenaded by Jacobson and Andrea who had melodious voices. We were truly in a paradise and not for one moment did I not realize this. When, if ever again, would I be so close to such lovely young women?

My desire and impulse of the moment was to take bewitching Ramon in my arms. But this was not to be. There were four of us men and all love starved and there were only three women. which made it complicated and frustrating. Thus, as all of us were officers and gentlemen, the fair ladies were driven back to Thio, and we said: "Good night and thank you for the wonderful evening."

Soon we dropped into wonderfully soft beds in the old Madam's hotel. It had been a glorious day and an enchanting evening I would never forget. Only one thing would have been nicer I thought. And that was to have the adorable Ramon in my arms.

The lusty crowing of a rooster aroused me from my dream of Ramon. As I lay in my soft bed I looked out over the sleeping village. I would have been content to stay here forever; but the War had other plans for me. We had to catch our plane by one o'clock. So Jacobson, Dreamer Fearon, and I aroused ourselves most reluctantly. Then we took our last fond look out over our dream village in Paradise and reluctantly headed westward up and out of the green valley.

Every moment of our exciting journey over the snake-like one-way road was etched into our minds forever. I feasted hungrily on the exotic tropical scenery, the dark green of the jungle and the lighter green of the niaoli trees forests. At the summit we left our valley of dreams and descended rapidly to the world of war and grim reality.

There had been no signs of soldiers or military life on the east Thio side of the mountains. In great contrast on the west side soldiers were everywhere. The Virgin's breast Mountain reached toward the sky. This was a shapely mountain which was famous as a landmark and a beautiful monument to all virgins.

The Dreamer and I were too early for our transport plane, so we stopped at the Tontouta River for a cool plunge into the deep and rapidly flowing water. Then, at the airfield, we ate a meal, packed our gear into the sturdy plane, and for the second time in my life I was flying. Our big DC-3 plane circled slowly over the field, gained altitude, then turned eastward. We crossed deep gorges and forests which I had not yet explored. Then down below we saw the beautiful valley we had so recently climbed in the Jeep.

Over this we flew where I took my last fond look at the enchanting home of Ramon, Loulette, and Andrea, our lovely new friends we had so reluctantly left behind us forever. Then we were over the majestic ocean. Great coral reefs protected New Caledonia from enemy submarines and the many violent cyclones. Many shades of blue and green water indicated the depth. The light green water was a sign of coral reefs, while the deeper blue was over deeper water.

It was a beautiful sunny day; a few puffy cumulus clouds mushroomed skyward over the great expanse of deep blue Pacific Ocean water. Soon we were over the flat Coraline Loyalty islands. Here below was a beachcomber's paradise. I vowed I'd visit these islands some day. It is claimed that a beautiful breed of women live on these three main islands. The fanatical Scots missionaries sired many babies from the Melanesian women. I was a believer in making dreams come true. In 1992, on a two months' epic return to New Caledonia, I took a stormy passage on a small inter-island freighter out of Noumea to Lifou the middle island of the Loyalties. I was given generous hospitality at a Protestant Mission station at the capital town of We. I swam at one of the most beautiful beaches in the world, and toured the mysterious coral island with the kind missionary where once cannibals had lived and where there had been a religious war between the Catholic and Protestant converts to Christianity with French troops involved.

An hour later the countless wild jungled islands of the New Hebrides came into view. These were reputed to be some of the wildest and least explored islands of the vast Pacific. The primitive-living Melanesian natives were still cannibals and head hunters. They called their victims who went into their cooking pots long pig.

Never before had I seen such a rugged looking jungle. Most of the coastline was rocky though there were small patches of white sand beaches fringed by tall palms. As we soared over this green no white man's land, I regretted I could not now explore it at a leisurely pace rather than going to Guadalcanal to an uncertain fate.

At the northern end of this chain of islands was Espiritu Santo, the largest and most cultivated of the islands. This island was flat and covered with dense jungle and great waving palm trees of the plantations. Soon we saw war ships anchored in a harbor and then an airfield. Our plane circled low over the field and made a perfect landing between long avenues of palms. A driver in a military truck picked us up and we were given quarters in a transit officers' camp. We didn't know if we were to move on to the Solomons that night or in a few days. I hoped it would be in a few days as I wanted some time to explore the island and collect zoological specimens. I was in no hurry to get to the dreaded islands of almost sure death—Guadalcanal.

The jungle was alive with thousands of shrill voices of insects and the humid air filled our lungs. Groaning and slopping through thick mud our truck arrived at the camp. We dumped out our gear and headed for the coral beach which was jagged and treacherous from the beating from great tropical storms. Myriads of tiny hermit crabs in their stolen sea shell houses crawled out of our way. We waded out on the coral and let the sea roll its cool water over us. To venture beyond the reef would be suicide for man-eating sharks swarmed in abundance in their hunger for human flesh and blood.

Darkness fell like a wet blanket over the singing jungle. We groped our way to the mess hall where we saw groups of fighting men soon on their way or back from the battle front on Guadalcanal. I was one of them now for I too was on the way to that little-known island which had so recently become so important in American history. The rough food in the mess hall tasted good and bolstered our spirits and was plentiful. Here at least we didn't have to line up to get our food as we were obliged to do on the old tub Argonne staff ship of ComSoPac with her gold braided snobs of Halsey's mostly Annapolis officers—Boys Towners as we reserves called them.

There was nothing to do now in the dark night but to go to bed. We were provided with cots in a well-screened Quonset hut to ward off the deadly malarial mosquitoes. We got the word that at one o'clock we were to be ready to move out to the front lines. I slept peacefully. The closer I got to the fighting zone the better I slept and the calmer I became.

Never would I forget being awakened in the middle of the night to go on the most thrilling plane ride in all my life. Five of us got our gear and were driven off in a reconnaissance car. We were given a hasty and bumpy ride over the muddy road to the airfield. There we were hurriedly pushed into a DC-3 plane; and before we realized it were off the ground and over the black jungle. In a few moments we were over the sea and on our way to the Solomons.

While my comrades slept, I lay awake to try to think and to look out to the glory of the Southern Cross, Orion, and the fleecy clouds into which our plane pushed its way like a giant bird. I had no desire to sleep nor did I have any fear. What was to happen was to happen. Anything I could do now wouldn't have the least affect on my fate. I had blind faith in my Guardian Spirit. I was thinking mostly of a young and beautiful girl I had come to love in my imagination. I thought how wonderful it would be if I could show this dream girl the wonders of nature I was seeing. I vowed to live that dream some day if I ever came back from Guadalcanal.

My half subconscious existence was pleasant and gave me comfort. We had all drunk some potent and awful rot gut brew we'd taken with us from New Caledonia and stuck it in our duffel bags. We were drunk and a bit paralyzed. I slept for a little while then awakened and became startled as I looked out upon the most thrilling and most spectacular sunrise I'd ever seen. We were flying about 10,000 feet over the sea and high over many clouds. The colored rays of the sun were reflected from clouds of many sizes and shapes. It was like entering the gates of Heaven and fully as thrilling. I gazed speechless and spellbound and was intensely happy. I was so involved in my sight seeing that the thought of encountering any Jap fighter planes was furtherest from my mind.

It was not long before I saw the first of the Solomon Islands, San Cristobal. She was blanketed with dense jungle of solid dark green cut by numerous bays and mountains. Neither warring nation had as yet bothered to occupy this majestic island in force. Our steadily droning plane sped on over Sealark Channel between Guadalcanal and Malaita and Florida island between them where some of the greatest sea battles in the world at this time were being fought almost every day.

At sunrise our plane circled then landed safely on Henderson field so recently carved out of coconut palm plantations by Korean labor forces of the Japanese. All was quiet until a truck came out to meet us. Some more trucks and men appeared. Our plane was quickly loaded with wounded men who were badly burned and suffering. Through long avenues of tall palms we were driven to the Navy encampment. In every directions we saw army tents and fox holes.

We now reported to our new commanding officer Lt. Commander Lincotus who promptly looked after us. Three of our group of five were to be sent over to Tulagi. Ed Fearon, Morris Baldwin, and I immediately responded to this request. where I imagined Jap bombers would seldom appear to bother us just 20 miles north over Sealark Channel.

As we would not leave until the next day, we were free to do what we pleased and within the limited American zone as yet held by our forces. We first visited a deep dugout of 40 feet under a hill. The battle bloodied Lunga River tempted us for a visit. There we had a cooling swim in spite of crocodiles said to be there. On the far shore I talked to Marines manning an antiaircraft position. After the swim and visit with the young Marines I went out to look around and to visit soldiers and to hear some of their tall tales of combat. I saw dozens of wrecked planes and shell and bomb craters now filled with water from torrential daily rains. A large fleet of Jap ships had been down a few weeks before to blast the airfield. A young Marine who appeared a bit out of his head bragged to me how many Jap planes had been shot down by his battery. He claimed they had the world's record for shooting down planes. His wild story was that his battery had shot down 800 planes. I immediately made it my ambition to collect the wild stories whether they were true or not.

Now I delivered a note to a young Marine fighter pilot who had just shot down two Jap planes. He was a very handsome nice fellow who's girl friend Ramon Hill of Thio I'd so recently been with. I wished him good luck in hunting

Jap planes, and to this very day of September 28th, 2000, I hope he survived the war and got back to lovely sexy Ramon.

While on my day of liberty on Guadalcanal, I drank coconut milk, rested in a tent for new arrivals, then looked around for supplies I could use from a kind Army quartermaster. He gave me a pair of shoes, and a free haircut I had from a Philippino messboy. I was now all set for going to my new duty assignment over on Tulagi.

Someone now told me to expect a daily arrival of a lone Jap twin-motored bomber. This character was known as Washing Machine Charlie as his plane sounded like an old washing machine the way it sputtered. He was a nuisance raider who would fly around at night keeping everyone awake and in a fox hole. Before he departed he would drop his 100-pound personnel bomb. He was one annoying character. Later we had Black Cat planes which would pursue Charlie as our anti-aircraft guns would blaze away at him. Charlie seldom did any serious damage; he was just an annoying trouble-maker.

I went to my army cot early and that lucky night Washing Machine Charlie didn't fly overhead nor Louie the Louse or Millimeter Mike didn't shoot artillery shells down into our camp.

November 30th, 1942.

It was raining off and on at Guadalcanal. I lay around considerably taking life as easy as much like a beachcomber as one could be in a nasty war. The word was getting around that a big Jap naval force was on the way down to land troops on Guadalcanal. According to coast watchers on Solomon Islands to the north there were ten war ships headed our way. Just off the beach the cargo ship Alchiba was burning from a Jap torpedo. In the afternoon everyone was very excited and getting ready for the visit of the Jap fleet.

At 5:30 p.m. Lt. J.G. Morris Baldwin, Lt. J.G. Ed Fearon, and I took passage on a motor torpedo boat (PT), and had a thrilling ride across the 20 mile wide Lango and Sea Lark channel, to Tulagi. The young PT boat skipper was Larson, a Swede from my home state of Minnesota. He was not a relative even though I had countless Swede Larson relatives in Minneapolis and many parts of Minnesota.

Upon arriving at the British government wharf at Tulagi, we were moved into the officers' quarters at a badly bombed out building up a hill from the Navy landing. After chow of spam, bread, and dehydrated potatoes, we went to bed on Army cots. About 11 p.m. Father Fitzgerald, a young Irish Catholic chaplain woke us up so we could witness a big naval battle. We went up a little hill to watch the coming drama. I hadn't seen a naval battle since I'd been in the Battle of Pearl Harbor. I was very excited and hoped it would be a sorely needed victory for our Navy. Father Fitzgerald had gotten the word about the battle from our radio station where I was assigned for duty the next day.

At 11: 20 p.m. we saw a cannon shell streaking in a high arch over the water heading southwestward. Then a few moments later more shells streaked a blazing trail through the dark night. How thrilling! Two big ships now began pouring out the red hot lead. Soon the air was full of flares lighting up the sky. We had no idea about the identity of the ships. The apposing fleets were really shooting at each other now. Two ships were burning savagely, then other ships also caught fire. We thought one Jap ship had burst into flames. We imagined or hoped it was a Jap ammunition ship. Of course it was all wishful thinking on our part for we had no way of knowing whose ships were being hit theirs or ours. A huge puff of flame rose about 1000 feet into the air. After about 20 minutes of battle, it was all over. I went back to bed as I imagined I'd witnessed a great American Navy victory. Things were going to be very interesting I could see.

December lst, 1942

In the early morning our heavy cruisers began to limp into Tulagi harbor. This great sea battle I was to learn was the Battle of Tassafarango and was another sorry defeat for us. The cruiser Northampton had been sunk. The USS Minneapolis, New Orleans, and the Pensacola had barely made it back to the safe haven of Tulagi harbor. We lost no destroyers in this battle. I was told that the Japs had lost seven or eight destroyers and transport ships. This optimistic report was all false scuttlebutt and most wishful hoping on our part.

Our cruisers were really in bad shape but luckily still afloat. We had two air raid alarms in the morning but no Jap planes appeared. I hiked around the island for awhile to observe the great battle scars from the pre-invasion bombardment by our planes and ships. There was wreckage all over the small island, and shell holes and bomb craters, and badly shattered buildings.

I saw men carrying buckets of arms and legs and other parts of bodies of our dead men which had been taken out of blasted gun turrets which had been blasted by Jap shells I'd seen soaring through the night sky. What a sad sight—all those poor dead Navy men which were being taken to a little cemetery and laid out side by side into a long trench. Chaplain Fitzgerald was praying over the bodies. This young handsome Catholic chaplain had so many marines die in his arms that he was really wild and out of his head. Also I remember he could tell naughty jokes to cheer us up.

Now I had a big surprise to see Navy Reserve Lt. Herb Fairchild, who had been head of my watch at CinCPac staff. He had been on the Minneapolis and was now shaking and white as a ghost. He had really gone through holy hell in the savage battle. It made me also think how lucky I could be. Fate had spared me from deadly ship duty serving on one of these blasted cruisers. I felt sorry for poor Herb who so recently had lorded it over me on his duty watch in communications back at Pearl Harbor.

I had been quickly introduced to Tulagi and the real war which up to this point was so different from the happy-go-lucky duty in New Caledonia on ComSoPac staff on the USS Argonne. Before I continue on with my journal account I will present chapters on the geography, history, and the August 7th battle on the taking of Tulagi.

3

The Geography of Guadalcanal, Savo, Florida And Tulagi

Before I begin the story of my wartime life on the island of Tulagi which I have given the name of Hell's Kitchen, I place it first in the larger context of the other Solomon islands which came into my area of sight and travels. The Guadalcanal campaign which included Tulagi, Florida, and Savo islands were of great significance in American history for it was there where the American armed forces in vicious fighting, turned back the evil Empire forces of Japan which had previously thought they were invincible.

As few people in America knew anything about the remote and distant Solomon Islands, I will briefly describe its geographical setting according to David Harcombe the author of SOLOMON ISLANDS, A TRAVEL SURVIVAL KIT. I thank him for his excellent research that produced so much excellent detail about the Solomon islands' past and its present place in the vast Pacific Ocean world.

According to Harcombe (1968, Page 7) the Solomons are the third largest archipelago in the South Pacific and covers over 800,000 square Kilometers of sea. It is made up of scattered double chain of 992 islands, atolls, and cays, which vary from those islands which are rugged, heavily wooded and mountainous, to tiny low lying coral atolls. The total land area is 29,785 square kilometers. These consist of six large islands and 30 smaller islands of wartime significance.

The six largest islands are Guadalcanal, New Georgia, Malaita, Isabel, Choisel, and Christoval. In length they range from 80 and 171 kilometers, and from 25 to 50 kilometers in width. The six large islands lie between 156 degrees and 161 degrees west Longitude, and 6 degrees to 11 degrees north Latitude.

Mt. Makarakombu is 2447 meters in height on Guadalcanal, and is typical of most of the groups of islands mountains. These are for the most part igneous formations overlain with ancient marine sediment. A dense rain forest covers most parts of the high islands, and mangrove swamps grow along many parts of the coasts. Coral reefs and lagoons have formed around many islands, and also many have formed around volcanic cones which have long since were overlain with level-topped terraces of coral rock. Some islands are former reefs lifted high out of the water by volcanic activity.

As part of the Pacific Ring of Fire, the Solomons volcanic area is at the intersection of the large Indo-Australian and Oceanic tectonic plates. These as they press vigorously together, cause constant seismic activity with earthquakes, and volcanoes. There are three land volcanoes and two submarine ones in the area of the islands. Savo island, near Guadalcanal, has numerous bubbling and boiling springs. Its crater blew off its top last time in 1840, and seismologists constantly keep an eye on it.

GUADALCANAL

According to Harcombe's description (1988, P.68), Guadalcanal is the largest of the Solomon islands, and is 160 kilometers long and 48 kilometers wide. It consists of a north-west to south-east mountainous spine which lies close to the southern weather coast. The interior of the island is forbidding, with many sheer and rugged mountains. The two highest peaks are Mt. Makarakomba (2447 meters), and Mt. Popomanaseu (2449 meters). Characteristic of the highland areas are mountains with sheer steep-sided narrow valleys. On the north-east coast these mountains descend into wide alluvial plains fed by shallow rivers and thickly planted with coconut groves.

At the north-west corner of the island quiescent volcanic cones rise to 1000 meters, while much of the south shore is backed by almost vertical cliffs. Cut by deep gorges, the central highlands are difficult to reach and are very hard to cross. The island's rivers are short and prone to flash-flooding. Treacherous off shore currents, fierce seas and strong undertows make the island's anchorages hazardous for small craft and especially so on the south coast.

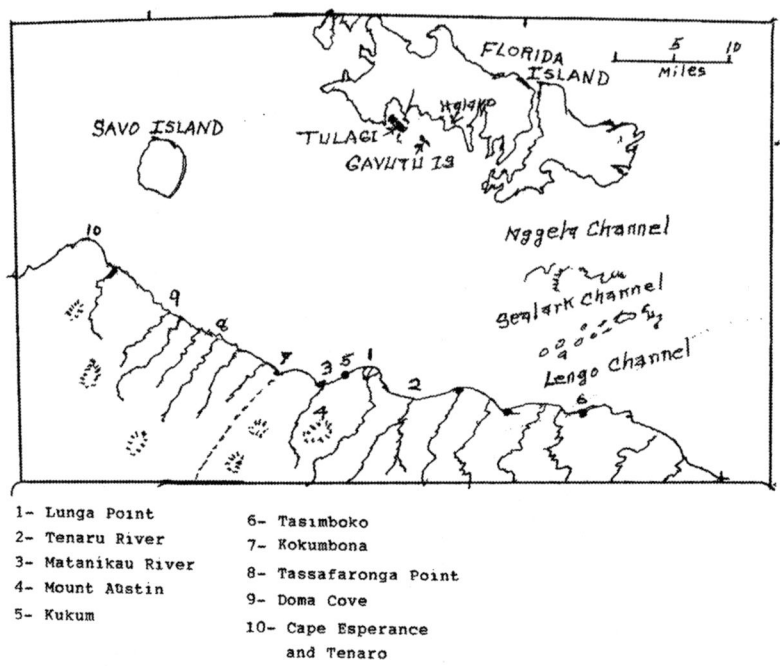

1- Lunga Point
2- Tenaru River
3- Matanikau River
4- Mount Austin
5- Kukum
6- Tasimboko
7- Kokumbona
8- Tassafaronga Point
9- Doma Cove
10- Cape Esperance and Tenaro

SAVO ISLAND

Many were the times in late afternoons while I was stationed on Tulagi, I would look off to the west to view the distant Savo Island in the midst of a beautiful sunset. It was a mysterious circular island where off its shore infested with hungry sharks so many of our ships and men were lost as well as those of the Japanese.

Harcombe only briefly describes Savo (1988, Page 103), as an active volcano with a pair of craters one of which encloses the other. The crater is 485 meters high and included along its rim are two hot springs. The famous island has 31 square kilometers which is 13 kilometers from northern Guadalcanal. Coconut groves almost encircle the island and a tractor trail near the shore goes all the way around it. The population of 2500 Melanesians live in 14 main villages. Their Papuan language is called Savosavo, and is similar to that of the nearby Russell islanders. Many small rivers flow down the central slope at the base of the crater.

THE NGGELA ISLANDS

During the war the islands of Nggela-Sula and Nggela-Pile were known as Florida Island. The largest of these two—Sula—sheltered the small island of Tulagi which will be described last. The Nggela islands are described as being over 36 kilometers long and consisting of 4 larger islands and about 50 smaller islands of various sizes. The two largest islands are divided by a long channel called Mboli Passage. This passage led to the north from Purvis Bay which was the WW II fleet anchorage and which was well protected by the encircling land. West of the narrow passage is Nggela Sula while Nggela Pile lies to the east. Up to the northwest of these Florida main islands lie Sandfly and Buena Vista. The Nggela islands are quite rugged; and in many places have towering eroded cliffs rising out of the sea. Many of the small islands have beautiful white coral beaches.

Nggela Sule island is thickly wooded with few native trails, and has very little population except along the northern coast from Anuha island to Mboli Passage. Also there are a few small villages opposite Tulagi. Up in the jungle from Mbola are some interesting caverns. One of these is called the Watering Hole from which a pipeline for fresh water was laid down all the way to Purvis Bay. A larger cave beyond the Watering Hole is a cave called the Cathedral. It is 15 meters high and is a home for many bats among its dripping Stalactites.

To the north of Nggela Sule (Florida Island) is the beautiful 70 hectare island of Anuha with sand beaches in a deep blue coral lagoon. Here in recent years was built the country's principal international resort which had the most ideal location for diving. To the northwest of Florida Island are Sandfly and Buena Vista islands. They have many fine beaches.

The Nggela Pile island to the east of Mboli Passage has a coastal track from the Melanesian Mission at Siota as far as Ndende with many sand beaches along the route. The tiny island of Laghale is three kilometers to the north of Ghate on Nggula Pile. Along the path from Ghale to Toa are the Talama caves and the Suku caves, then further along this trail are the Mbambana caves.

TULAGI

At last we come to the small island which in WW II became known to many U.S. Servicemen who were stationed there as Hells' Kitchen. While the British used the spelling of this famous war-torn island as Tulaghi, the Solomon islanders pronounced it as Tu-lang-ie. It is about roughly two miles long and half a mile wide, and lying south and west of Florida Island. A ridge rising over 300 feet above the sea marks the northwest-southeast axis of the island. About half of the way down from the northwest tip of Tulagi the ridge is broken by a ravine and then rises again in a triangle of hills to the southernmost which was designated as Hill 281 which is its height.

Along the shore of the northeast part of Tulagi are mangrove thickets beyond Sasape. Along the shore of the northwest part of the island is a reef where the money cowry seashells can be found growing in abundance. The reef of coral formation plunges off into deep water. Most of the northern part of the island is covered with jungle.

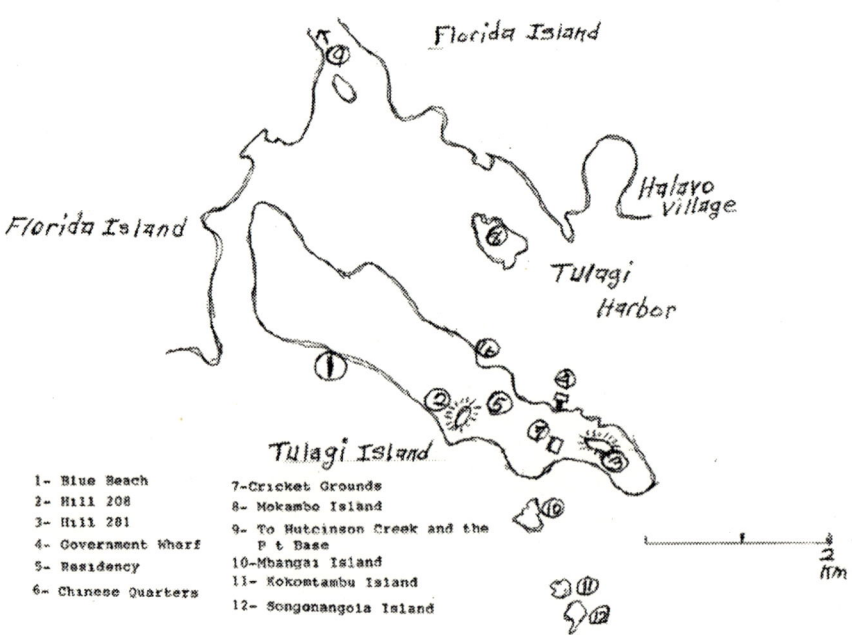

1- Blue Beach
2- Hill 208
3- Hill 281
4- Government Wharf
5- Residency
6- Chinese Quarters
7- Cricket Grounds
8- Mokambo Island
9- To Hutchinson Creek and the P t Base
10- Mbangai Island
11- Kokomtambu Island
12- Songonangola Island

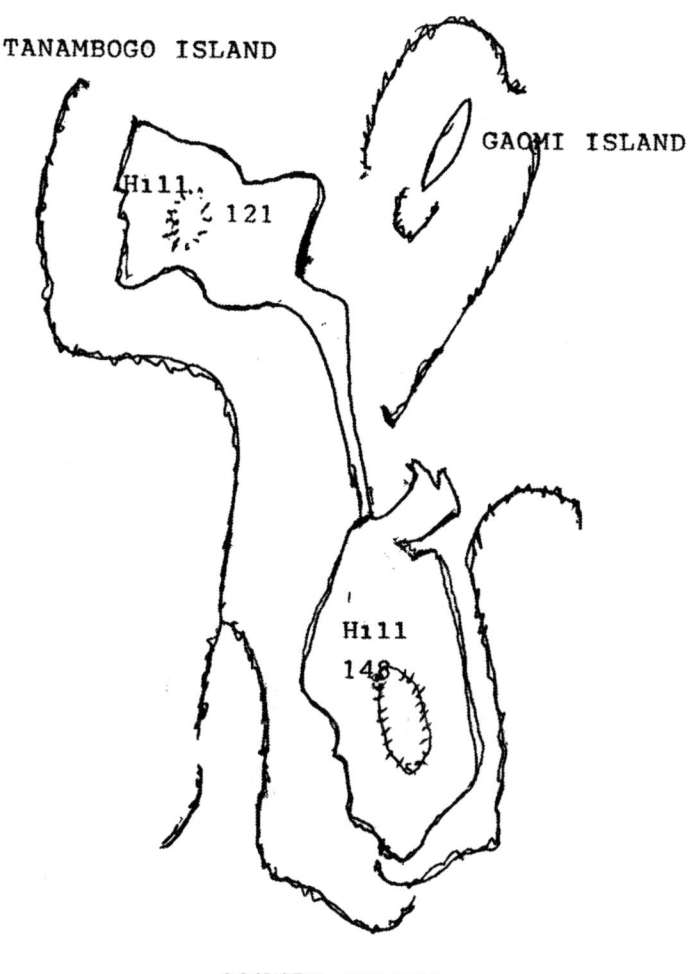

THE CLIMATE OF THE SOLOMONS

The tropical climate is tempered by the surrounding ocean. During the islands' winter from April to early November, the southeast trade winds bring mild weather. The frequent rain squalls are short and usually several days apart.

Even though winter is the calmest season, strong winds often blow up to as much as 50 kilometers per hour and can last for as long as ten days at a time and bring heavy rainfall. This occurs especially in July along Guadalcanal's southern weather coast.

During the summer months from mid-November to mid-April monsoon winds usually come from the west and northwest. This is the Solomon's wet season and has higher temperatures, rainfall, and humidity. Characteristic of this season are short, sudden torrential cloudbursts followed by bright sparkling sunshine. Beautiful sunsets are almost. daily occurrences.

The coastal temperatures in the daytime are usually from 26 degrees C to 29 degrees C with the average being 31 degrees centigrade. The evening temperature may fall to 19 degrees C as the air is cooled by land breezes coming off nearby mountains and hills. The humidity is highest during mornings and gets up to 90%, then decreases in the afternoons. The humidity can fall off to 60% during the cooler months of the year over on the southern coast 492 inches a year often occurs-41 feet of rain. The high mountains there are almost always covered with rain clouds. The heavy rainfall in the Guadalcanal mountains produce many fast flowing rivers with waterfalls. Flash floods are frequent. The water in the rivers is of good quality except near native villages. Cyclones usually occur between January and April, and sometimes as early as November and as late as May. The strongest cyclones build up in the Coral Sea located south of the Solomons and move southward to Vanuatu, the Loyalties, New Caledonia, and Australia. They can do much damage to native villages constructed of native jungle materials.

4

A Brief History of Guadalcanal, Florida, Savo, And Tulagi Islands

According to Marcombe (Solomon Islands, p. 9), "Most historians believe Pacific Ocean peoples originated in South-East Asia. About 40,000 years ago, or perhaps earlier, they began to migrate through Indonesia and New Guinea toward Australia."

Before the early expanding populations of mixed Austrainesians and Papuan-speaking proto-Melanesians had moved into the Solomon Island chain, they had learned garden agriculture and the raising of pigs. This according to Harcombe, (P.9), was about 4000 B.C. and occurred in New Guinea which advanced them from hunter-gatherers to primitive farmers.

By 2000 B.C. the dynamic Lapita cultural people appeared on the scene. These people of Melanesian extraction took their name from an archaeological site at Lapita in New Caledonia. In 1994 when I visited New Caledonia, I saw the Lapita markings on rock faces in a mountain stream valley near Poya in central New Caledonia. Their distinctive pottery has been discovered widely scattered from the Bismarck Archipelago of Eastern New Guinea all the way to Samoa and in the Solomons as far as Tikopia. It is believed this culture became extinct by 800 A.D. the time of noticeable decline occurred.

In the Solomons by this time most of the Melanesian peoples were living in small villages on tribal lands, were practicing shifting agriculture, were fishing, hunters, and were good craftsmen and canoe-builders, and conducted feasts and dancing ceremonies, The extended family tribal groups raided their neighbors, and were widely ruled by tribal elders. They practiced ancestor worship, blood feuds, head-hunting, and cannibalism.

Small groups of sea-going Polynesians reached the fringes of the Solomons and settled only on the isolated islands and atolls while the Melanesians lived on the heavily forested big islands. They eliminated or absorbed the new comers. From the 13th to the 17th centuries, the warlike Tongans raided the Solomons peoples. Because of these raids the Solomon Islanders became suspicious of all foreigners and often would attack ocean-going peoples from Polynesia. The Spaniards in the early 1500s in Peru were hearing from Inca legends about gold, silver and slaves from islands of the Solomon groups. It was also believed that there was a great southern continent which gave balance to the land masses of the Northern hemisphere. Don Alvaro de Mendana Neyra was chosen to find these legendary islands and the great southern continent. His mission was to establish a colony there and convert the inhabitants to Christianity.

Leaving Peru in two ships on November 19th, 1567, he sighted land at Tuvalu, then at Ontong Java, and then at the large island of Santa Isabel which he named. He returned to Peru and claimed there was great wealth on his newly discovered islands. He named the islands Yslas su Llamen de Salomon. He discovered Santa Cruz and settled there on a second expedition. Due to the islander hostility, sickness, and his death from malaria, the survivors returned to Peru. After Pedro Fernandez de Queros led an expedition in 1606 in search of Tierra Australia, he did discover Espiritu Sanboin the New Hebrides. This island became an important Allied base in WW II. His failure to make more important discoveries among the Solomon Islands, led to Spain's losing interest in that part of the Pacific.

The Solomon Islands became lost to the European exploration nations for 161 years after the failures of Quiros. Then in 1767 two Dutch expeditions saw Ontong Java two times. Captain Cartaret an Englishman, in 1767 saw Nendo and continued on to Malaita. He was followed by British and French expeditions. One of these in 1788 was Captain Shortland on his way home after accompanying a fleet of convict ships to colonize Australia.

It is believed whalers made unrecorded trips to the Solomons from 1820 to 1840. These were followed by traders in search of sandalwood, tortoise shell, and pearl shell as trade goods for even more sandalwood for the China trade. The restless traders brought European diseases to the islanders who had no immunity. Also their treachery to the natives caused them to attack foreigners and to murder some European missionaries. The Solomons soon gained the reputation as being populated by fierce warlike and cannibalistic savages.

According to Harcombe (1988, P. 11) by 1860 the much desired trade goods of traders gave them a foothold in some safer villages in the Solomons. The introduction of firearms led to a greatly increased growth to head-hunting and slave raiding.

In the later part of the 19th century black birding shipped nearly 19,000 Solomon Islanders to Queensland in Australia, and 10,000 to Fiji to work on sugar plantations. The cruelty of the black birders created hatred for the Europeans among the Solomon Islanders.

THE SOLOMON ISLAND PROTECTORATE

Britain by 1893 had proclaimed the southern part of the Solomons as their protectorate and became known as the British Solomon Islands Protectorate. The main interest of the Protectorate officials was to keep law and order, stop the head-hunting and cannibalism, and to prevent the exploitation of the natives.

The first Resident Commissioner in 1896 was Charles Morris Woodford who it was claimed was to become a most remarkable man. He controlled 100,000 Solomon Islanders with only the help of a few other Europeans and a small local force of police. As a man who never carried a gun, he tried to convince the islanders of the futility of tribal warfare and head-hunting. By 1915, when he retired, he had established a good foundation for organized government in the islands.

As government money was scarce education and health was left to the many competing missions who claimed their version of Christianity to be correct and all the others wrong. The islanders had much of their traditional customs and way of life eroded by the proselytizing soul savers. However to their credit sorcery, warfare, and head-hunting diminished, and health improved. Over on wild Malaita highland tribesmen rebelled against paying a tax by foreign governments they did not want, and often killed tax collectors.

WORLD WAR II

From Harcombel's good short summary of the next part of Solomon Island history (1988, P. 12) I quote: "The otherwise settled, peaceful pattern of life in the Solomons was completely shattered in 1942." In the Shortland Islands in early April, the Japs invaded. Then at Tulagi, the British Colonial capital, was captured by them three weeks later.

Typical of these sadistic and cruel people at that period in their history, they disgraced themselves as invaders of innocent native peoples. They robbed the churches, demolished food from the natives at gun point, stole clothes and other property, and forced adult males to work for no wages. They looted gardens which destroyed the natives ability to support themselves. Soon the natives feared, hated, and avoided these cruel Jap invaders.

It wasn't long before US reconnaissance planes noticed an airfield being constructed on Guadalcanal. The island would have to be captured before the Japs next headed for the New Hebrides, New Caledonia, and Australia and New Zealand. It was then on August 7th, 1942, that the U.S. Marines landed on Guadalcanal, Florida and Tulagi Islands.

After more than six months of savage fighting on land and the sea, the U.S. forces conquered the Jap invaders and destroyed their false self image of invincibility as they secretly withdrew to other Solomon islands to the northwest.

It was estimated that as many as 40,000 islanders lost their life in World War II from starvation and the fighting all around them. The loyalty of the Solomon Islanders for the Allied cause was great. They served on their own scouting and guerilla operations against Jap patrols; they rescued shot-down Allied aviators. They assisted coast watchers behind Jap lines. Some islanders were decorated for their bravery and heroic service toward Allied victory. Many islanders came to Guadalcanal to serve as laborers, orderlies and porters at the large U S supply base on Guadalcanal. These days were great for the islanders as the generous Americans paid them as much as four times more than the pre-war British wages.

HISTORY OF TULAGI ISLAND

This small island lying close to Florida Island was originally chosen as the colonial capital because of its central position in the Solomon Island chain and because of its fine deep water harbor. In 1897 Tulagi became the Protectorate capital. Then in 1910 the Burns Philip Company opened a store there. Soon to follow them the Chinese boat builders established themselves there; and the British government opened a hospital.

At the time of the Kwaio native rebellion on Malaita, Tulagi's population was 1,000. However, at that time there were only 35 government officials in all the Protectorate over 95,000 native inhabitants and 30 of these lived on Tulagi. Before the Japanese invasion the panic-stricken European officials and some of the missionaries fled Tulagi. On August 7th, 1942, US Marines invaded and quickly recaptured the island, and a few days later the well dug in Japs on nearby Gavutu and Tanamboga islands were defeated.

After Tulagi had been captured, a Naval base was established with a secure harbor refuge for Allied shipping. A P.T. base was established along Hutchinson Creek on Florida Island. A seaplane base was established at Gavutu and at Halavo on Florida Island. On Tulagi a radio station was soon operating. Construction battalion units moved in and a base hospital was soon in operation. A Naval wharf got into operation as the housing for the Base Commander's office. Nearby was the supply base. Over at Purvis Bay on Florida Island served as a large Fleet refuge and assembly place for our ships. But after the war the badly damaged Tulagi was not considered worth reconstructing it to become the capital which was established over on Guadalcanal on the famous battlefield of World War II. The new town of Honiara became the country's capital built on the blood-soaked sacred ground of the long battle back in 1942 and 1943.

SAVO ISLAND

In 1568 the members of the Spaniard Mendala's expedition saw Savo island volcano erupting and named it Sasarga. In 1840 there was another eruption of the volcano with much loss of life. The warriors of Savo Island in the 1870s were on head-hunting raids mostly at the neighboring Russell Islands. It also was one of the first of the Solomon islands to have a European trader.

After 1899, when Savo's population was estimated to be about 4,000, epidemics of European diseases had greatly reduced the island's population. By 1970 the population was 1,300.

Savo's greatest time of its history was to come on August 9th, 1942, while the landing of U.S. troops and their supplies were coming ashore on Guadalcanal. A Jap naval force slipped out of Rabaul, and headed toward Guadalcanal. In spite of their sighting by an American submarine, a Flying Fortress, and an Australian Hudson pilot, the U.S. fleet in the area had not taken warning.

The U.S. heavy cruisers and one Australian cruiser guarding the supply operations and troop ships off Guadalcanal were taken by surprise in a night battle called the Battle of Savo Island.

The American cruisers Quincy, Astoria, and Vincennes were sunk, the Chicago badly damaged, and the HMAS Canberra sunk. This was the greatest U.S. Naval defeat in her history. Luckily the Jap commander did not press on to destroy the U.S. supply and transport ships but played safe and retired. Many other naval battles were fought off Savo Island which became part of the history of the Guadalcanal campaign. Many survivors from the sunken ships were savagely attacked by the pro-Japanese sharks in the water.

5

The Battle for Tulagi, Gavutu, And Tanambogo

What was the physical condition of Tulagi when Ed Fearon, Morris Baldwin, and I arrived there on December 1st, 1942? The islands had been severely pounded by our ships and from the air by our planes. Wreckage littered the islands as most of the British government buildings had been hit and were in bad condition for the use of the American Naval base.

The islands would be my home until November of 1943. Before I continue my story taken from my diary account written on British Solomon Island official paper I'd found scattered on the floor of the Residency, I will briefly describe the dramatic invasion by our Marine select troops.

From two accounts of the Tulagi battle (GUADALCANAL by Richard B. Frank, and GUADALCANAL 1942 by Joseph N. Mueller), I will describe the fierce fighting for the capture of my future Solomon Island station. Frank states: p. 72, "The Japanese garrisoned Tulagi with a detachment of the 3rd Kure Special Naval Landing force totaling 350 men under Commander Masaaki Suzuki." American aerial reconnaissance revealed that the northeast and southeast beaches fronted the strongest defenses

I now quote from Martin Clemen's from his book ALONE ON GUADALCANAL, p. 106–107. "First dawn broke cold and still. As the fingers of light picked out our sentries—huddled, nodding figures, keeping a weary watch—the vast white cumulus clouds over Guadalcanal suddenly came alive with the roar of planes, and the familiar heavy rumble of bombs began to be heard from Tulagi."

It was a carrier raid on the Japanese ships in Tulagi harbor. Great joy went out on the station drums as American torpedoes rained down on Japanese shipping in the harbor. Twelve dive bombers, then came another squadron of twelve bombers to keep attacking most of the morning. Fourteen Jap ships were limping out of the harbor. Some had been sunk and others were listing badly. Clemens was now over on Guadalcanal at Aola twenty miles from Tulagi. The Japanese Kawanisis patrol planes were patrolling regularly up and down along the coast while Clemens burned their last damaged Catalina seaplane.

Catholic Brother James Thrift from Mahina, brought along two American downed pilots from the carrier Yorktown. After three days on a rubber boat they had reached the south coast near Ave Ave. The pilot was Lt. Leonard H. Ewoldt, and his radioman was Ray Machalinski. They had observed five direct hits on ships in Tulagi harbor. Ewoldt had attacked a small cargo ship near Savo Island, and seen her go down along with two other Jap ships.

According to Lufe Schroeder who had a good view of the carrier plane attack, he had seen three light cruisers sink, and one of them near Mboli Passage, and the other two on reefs inside the harbor. Sharks had feasted on hundreds of Jap bodies floating in the water after their ships had been sunk. The small islands in and near Tulagi harbor had been occupied by the Japs. These were Tanambogo, and Gavutu and Makambo.

Some AIF detachment men were still in Tulagi Harbor when the Japs had arrived. In the approaching darkness they slipped away after they had demolished installations which could be of use to the enemy. They claimed hundreds of Japs had been killed during the American air raid. There were still, according to observers, from seven to eight hundred Japs still on Tulagi and the harbor islands. It was now up to the Americans to get rid of these Japanese military personnel and occupy Hells Kitchen Tulagi, my future home.

On August 7th, 1942, Tulagi was occupied by the 3rd Kure Special Naval Landing force of about 350 men under the command of Mosaaki Suzuki. The strongest Jap defenses fronted the northeast and southeast beaches on Tulagi. The Marines selected a 500-yard long strip of shore about midway on the southwest side of the island for their assault. This was to become known as Beach Blue.

The invasion force under Captain George B. Ashe on the U.S.S. Neville, anchored 5 miles off the beach. Rupertus's Landing Force was of the 1st Raider Battalion, the 1st Battalion 2nd Marines, and the 2nd Battalion 5th Marines, 3rd Marines, and the 1st Parachute Battalion.

The first American assault troops to land on Tulagi was Company B, 1st Battalion, 2nd Marines under Captain Edward J. Crane, They came ashore near Haleta on Florida Island at 0740 to secure a promontory which commanded Blue Beach. There they encountered no Japanese. The rest of this Battalion under Lt. Col. Robert B. Hill came ashore on Halavo on Florida Island and were not encountered by any Jap force. At 0800 Company B and D landed on the coral and came ashore. The lead companies drove straight across the island where

Company B secured Sasapi on the Tulagi Harbor side while Company D crested the spine of the island. A second wave landed Companies C and A. The Marines advanced down the island where their first resistance came from outposts in the Chinese quarters.

The Second Battalion of the 5th Marines under the command of Lt. Col. Harold E. Rosecrans landed on Blue Beach at 0916. They advanced through the northwest end of the island where they didn't encounter any Japanese.

The Raiders ran into heavy opposition when they tried to advance beyond Phase Line A. (See the map.) There was heavy machine gun fire coming from the southwest side of the spine around Hill 208. Company C overpowered all resistance then continued their advance with Company A until they reached a place where the ground dropped off to a small field which was the cricket grounds. One platoon of Company C reached the shore at the southeast tip of the island.

The Japs were well dug in in their dugouts and tunnels. Their defense tactics included allowing the point of a unit through, then they would ambush the main body and used their snipers to harass the Marines. But the Japs were poor marksmen.

As it was late in the day the Marines prepared a defense for the night. The Japs made savage counter attacks and drove a wedge between companies C and A. Small groups of Japs infiltrated as far as the Residency which would soon be my home. Some Japs got into the building but the Marines had departed from it. The next morning these Japs were slaughtered and left 26 dead close to the building. The toughest fighting was soon to come 3000 yards to the east of Tulagi on the islands of Gavutu and Tanambogo. These two were joined by a causeway. Gavutu had a hill 148 feet high; and the hill on Tanambogo was 121 feet high. Around the islands were coral reefs on the west side which made an amphibious approach only possible from the east side. The Jap defenders totaled 536 men which included 342 men of the Yokohama Air Group Landing Force who operated the seaplane base. There were 144 men of the 14th Construction Unit, and 50 men of a platoon of the 3rd Kure Special Naval Landing Force.

The Marines selected to take the two islands were the 1st Parachute Battalion under Major Robert H. Williams. They numbered only 397 men and were outnumbered by the defenders. The light cruiser San Juan and the destroyers Monssen and Buchanan blasted Gavutu for only five minutes while dive bombers from the aircraft carrier Wasp bombed the islands but did little damage.

The first wave of Marine attackers got to the concrete dock then advanced inland about 75 yards where Japs from the two hills poured in a concentrated fire on the Marines. Companies B and C. were heavily hit before they took a position in the damaged Lever Brother's store. Two staff officers were killed and the Battalion commander was wounded.

By 1400 Hill 148 on Gavutu was captured by members of Company B and some from Company A. By 1800 the American flag replaced the Jap colors on the hill. During the night some Japs came out from caves and dugouts to fight. Five boats set out for the northeast shore of Tanambogo, but were repulsed and the Americans suffered severe casualties. The boats were recalled taking many wounded men with them.

Turner released the remaining battalions of the reserve to continue attacking at Tulagi in the morning. the Marines advanced over Hill 281 to the southwest side of the island. Organized Jap resistance had ceased; but some fighting continued for four more days. Finally all the Japs who continued to fight were blasted out of caves. Only three Japs surrendered on Tulagi. Some had swum over to Florida Island where they were hunted down by Marine and native patrols.

At 1500 on August 8th the San Juan shelled Tanambogo; then the destroyer Buchanan pounded the island at short range. The Japs disabled a U.S. tank and set it afire as Marine riflemen shot 42 Japs around the flaming tank. A total of 122 Americans were killed in the taking of Tulagi, Gavutu, while 863 Japs were killed. Soon I would be living in the midst of all the wreckage.

6

For Me the Real War Begins

AT LAST I had the honor of getting into the shooting war and right on the front lines. Oh yes, I'd had one day of real war on December 7th, 1941, almost a year before. When the smoke and shock of that most unbelievable day had worn off and gone away, life for me had been pretty much of a glorious south seas island holiday. Living at Pearl Harbor with time off to explore beautiful Oahu and pursue lovely maidens had been a dream come true. Then for four months my fascinating life ashore on liberty and duty in New Caledonia had been a glorious experience.

Now, at last, I was a part of the Guadalcanal campaign—the first great land battle against the Japanese. The worst battles for possession for Guadalcanal had been won on land and at sea. But the battle would drag on for not yet had the Japs given up trying desperately to hang on and bring in reinforcements.

My habit of keeping a journal was a problem. We had Navy instructions that no diaries were to be kept because of the danger that these, if gotten into the hands of the enemy, could be of help to them. Luckily I was able to evade this order. As soon as I was settled into a badly damaged building on Tulagi, I began to explore the battered island. Up at the partially bombed residency on a hill overlooking the harbor, much to my delight, I was to find sheets of paper scattered all over the floor. These were the official papers of the British Solomon Islands Protectorate. What a gold mine. I gathered them up by the handfuls. I would keep my diary on these impressive and most historical sheets. To get around Navy censorships regulations I used these for letters which I never sent anywhere. I was later able to use them to write up my war time memoirs.

Thus far in the war I had been most fortunate. I'd only seen the killing from a distance. The only time I had requested duty was in Pearl Harbor at CinCPac when I'd volunteered to join ComSoPac staff located at that time in Auckland, New Zealand. But, my fate was in the hands of the Navy. I would be obliged to go where they sent me. The USS Argonne enroute to New Zealand out of Pearl

Harbor with me on it got orders enroute to go to Noumea in New Caledonia. ComSoPac Staff was to move their headquarters to that historical French colony.

Thus far in my Naval career I had been most fortunate. A Guardian Spirit seemed to watch over me. At Northwestern Midshipman school in Chicago I'd graduated exactly in the middle of my class of 1200 reserve midshipmen. All those below me had been flunked out. Then I'd weathered a great storm in sailing on a hundred and fifteen foot YP (Yacht Patrol) Boat to Pearl Harbor arriving two days before the infamous battle. I'd survived the Battle of Pearl Harbor, and arrived safely in Noumea harbor, and landed at Henderson Field on Guadalcanal after a flight over beautiful green jungle islands enroute. From my vagabond journey through America, Europe, and North Africa on a "shoe string" I'd developed a happy-go-lucky hang loose philosophy of life.

As I took a sheet of my salvaged British Government paper I wrote as follows: Subject: December 1st, 1942. My Life as a Beach Comber. I'd decided to give my journal writing this title because in spite of my often urgent work as a Navy Base communicator, I vowed I'd hang loose as much as possible as that attitude was much healthier than being an uptight duty-struck individual which was the attitude and behavior of many new young officer arrivals to Tulagi. Some of the "uptighters" were young men from broken homes in big cities. I'd had the good fortune of having my youth spent out in the beautiful forest and lake country around my home in northern Minnesota.

Now on this historical day of December 1st, 1942, I was determined to enjoy my wartime situation on this most historical south seas island as much as possible. Yes, I would call myself a beach comber. I'd read many great books by Stevenson, Jack London, and James Michener later. From these books I got of South Sea islands, scantily clothed maidens, romance, lovely palm lined beaches, and sailing on sail boats on enchanted seas.

The sight of so many Marines staggering around with malaria made me all the more determined to keep healthy and free of the fever if possible. In the afternoon I went on duty at the base radio shack. This was a wooden building on the side of a hill overlooking Tulagi harbor. Fox holes had been dug nearby and protected by stout coconut logs. When condition red sounded on a bell down by the Base head-quarters at the Navy landing wharf, we would head for the closest fox hole along the way.

Most of the radiomen were lucky survivors from the sunken aircraft carrier Hornet which was only about a year old. She was lost in the ill-fated Battle of Santa Cruz. Soon I would write of this most unfortunate battle in honor of my great radiomen. The young Naval Reserve officer in charge of communications was Lt. David Grace. He was an Ivy leaguer from the famous Grace line shipping family. With his political influence this handsome nice young man was soon to be returned to the States to take lighter than air training. He would fly a balloon and patrol off our east coast in search of German submarines.

As the communications staff had three new reserve officers, Ed Fearon, Morris Baldwin, and me, the watches were shorter. At this time the base was not much bothered with Washing Machine Charley.

That evening I talked with some Navy aviators. Some native Solomon Islanders employed by the Navy were living under our house and got about four times more pay than they had gotten from the British plantation owners and the Colonial Government. The Lever Brothers had their big plantations of coconut trees on the coastal flat lands on Guadalcanal where the Marines were camped and fighting the Japs. Some of the dusky Melanesian Islanders were employed as scouts who would go out on search parties over on nearby Florida Island to hunt down Japs who'd escaped Tulagi when the Marines had invaded.

That night of December second we were serenaded by cicadas. Just before the golden sun in a blaze of glory would sink behind Savo island, we would be serenaded by these musical insects. Their song was done by the rubbing of their wings. They gave a warning that soon we could expect Washing Machine Charlie to fly overhead. Condition RED would be rung and it was gunners to their anti-aircraft guns and it would be Fourth of July again with thousands of dollars being wasted with the shells that never hit Charlie.

December 3rd, 1942.   Thursday. For this day I entitled EXPLORING TULAGI.

On every Thursday natives would come to Tulagi with a great variety of fruits and nuts to trade with us. They would arrive in their picturesque alligator canoes. These frail craft of thin slats of wood stuck together with resin were black with a crocodile face and a tail which went straight up from four to five feet. The sides and, head and tail were beautifully inlaid with mother of pearl and white egg sea shells. The natives would trade for tobacco, spam, money, trinkets and clothes. A mean Marine officer, most likely an Annapolis "Boys' Towner" tried to stop this trading by some nasty regulation he'd dug up to kill joy of life. To avoid this duty struck officer, we would go over to Macambo Island out in the bay to trade for fruits, coconuts, some kind of nuts I'd never seen before. After walking around the island, I took a boat back to Tulagi, happily loaded down with loot.

That evening I heard from a Marine how a patrol of 20 Marines had killed seventeen Japs over on Florida Island. The poor bastards had been caught while they were having breakfast.

Before it was Washing Machine Charlie time, earlier in the day I was most fortunate in getting a ride in a harbor boat out to Gavutu and Tanambogo Islands where so many of our Marines had been killed while capturing the heavily defended islands. The trees were all shot down and wreckage was all over the place. Broken landing boats were at the water's edge. I then got a ride over to Florida Island on a Guard mail boat. There were about twenty Marines living in an old abandoned native village. It was a beautiful place under tall waving coconut palms. It had a white sand beach fringed by palm trees. I vowed to return here on a day of liberty as soon as possible. A Mr. Arnot of the United States Press was with me. I invited him to have dinner at our mess on Tulagi. He was a fine fellow and had a fascinating job as a war correspondent.

December 4th, 1942.   A TROPICAL RAIN STORM AND A NIGHT BATTLE.

I spent the day while not on watch at the radio shack decorating my room with pictures of beautiful American movie starlets such as my favorite Rita Haworth, then Jane Russell, Maria Montez and others. We were all love starved. I corresponded with a goodly number of nice girls back in the States and at Oahu in Hawaii. Young high school girls back in the states had been encouraged to write to military men fighting in a war zone. It was supposed to bolster our morale. One young lady in particular had stuck my fancy.

This young lady was a Miss Dorothy Ratcliffe from my home town at Aitkin in northern Minnesota. I'd last seen her when she was about fifteen years of age when I was a counselor at a Campfire girls camp. Now she was eighteen and had developed into a most attractive young woman. I'd already lost all hope for beautiful Harriet Shephardson back in Honolulu as she had so many young men hot after her. I'd been really smitten by Harriet so had put in for duty in Auckland, New Zealand in hopes the many adorable young ladies there could help me forget about Harriet. Well to get back to this Dorothy girl. I'd never dated her as I was all of seven years her elder. The photographs she sent me made me sit up and take notice. She was about five feet nine inches tall with a lovely figure, amber brown hair and I think greenish eyes. Her letters were rather innocent and didn't mention that she was "hot for my love and body" so I had to imagine what I wanted her to be. Yes, eager to get into bed with me for really wonderful love. Many of our American girls had been put on pedestals by their boys.

Some—yes—many of these adorable creatures got off the pedestals when most of the boys had gone off to war. I hopefully imagined this Dorothy, who'd gone off to Hollywood and became a messenger at Paramount Theatre Company, was fully as lovely as some of the pictures of ladies on my wall. I foolishly let my imagination run away from me.

We had a real tropical rain storm which cooled the air nicely. Late that night there was another battle out on Iron Bottom Sound. Our P.T. boats in late afternoon rumbled out of Hutchinson Creek then out of Tulagi Harbor. They were after some Jap destroyers unloading troops over on Guadalcanal. Later I heard that the P.T. boat skippers claimed they had hit three destroyers with torpedoes. Usually these claims were overly optimistic. I did see a ship burning way out at sea. Hopefully it was a Jap ship.

December 5th, 1942.   SEEING HERB FAIRCHILD.

Today I saw Lt. Herb Fairchild, the fellow who had been in charge of my watch section up at CinCPac in Pearl Harbor. Herb had lorded it over me and had been down right nasty to me at times. But also he had taught me a lot about Navy communications. He had luckily escaped his death while he was in the dreadful night battle of Tassaronga I'd witnessed the first day I was on Tulagi. He'd been on the heavy cruiser U.S.S. Chicago and not the Minneapolis I'd first mentioned. Poor Herb was still pale as a ghost from his ordeal.

I then hiked up to the other end of Tulagi which was separated only a short distance across a narrow channel to Florida Island. I was tempted to swim across but thought of possible salt water crocodiles and sharks though I didn't see any in the clear water. I waded out on a coral reef and much to my joy discovered many beautiful Money Cowry shells which I collected. The reef dropped off into very deep water. This end of Tulagi was unoccupied and had thick jungle growth on it. For a naturalist like me I could see the island was going to be very interesting.

Tulagi Island and Songonangona, Kokomtambu, and Mbangai Islands.
U.S. Navy photograph.

The town of Tulagi spared by the bombardment by US ships prior to the landing by Marines on August 7, 1942. US Navy Dept. photograph.

For Me the Real War Begins   45

US troops land on beach of Florida Island of the morning operations of
August 7th, 1942.

Island of Tulagi

US landing forces off Florida Island across the channel from Tanambogo on August 7th, 1942.

A Marine enjoying a shower on Guadalcanal. US Navy photograph.

For Me the Real War Begins

The great Sergeant Major Jacob Vouza who survived bayonet wounds by Jap soldiers. He led scouting patrols, rescued downed U.S. pilots behind enemy lines, and later was knighted and became Prime Minister of the new country after WWII.

US Marines coming ashore to Florida Islands on August 7th, 1942.

Marines on Guadalcanal lining up for a meal. Picture obtained from US National Archives in Washington DC.

Local Melanesians at Tulagi

Marine Chaplain Fitzgerald at a funeral ceremony on Tulagi after a great sea battle.

7

A Letter Home And Dengue Fever

A letter I dated January 4th on the Solomon Island Administration paper I quote as follows: Dear Home Folks:

Thought I would throw in a few lines here. My new boss at the Comm shack is a Lt. Comdr Wall (USNR) who comes from Milaca, Minnesota. His father and brother run a bottling works. We at first got along fine. I now have much more responsibility and for the first time I feel that I am actually contributing something for my country and the war effort.

Am taking life as easy as I can. I have to take care of my good health so I don't get the malaria which is laying low so many of our guys out here. We also have dysentery and dengue fever here. I take atabrine tablets to help prevent malaria and use neoli oil from New Caledonia to rub on my skin before I go to bed. So far so good. Have a cool room well decorated with pictures of America's most alluring women such as Rita Hayworth, Jane Russell, Sheila Johnson etc including pictures of two girls of my own who I think are equally beautiful. The family picture is right here on the front lines with me—with all their beaming faces.

I was sent up here because I was raising too much hell in the office down at ComSoPac down on the USS Argonne in Noumea. But instead of punishing me they did me a favor, for now I can collect hundreds of dollars worth of butterflies, seashells, and wild orchid bulbs.

Yesterday I visited an abandoned native village on an island near us which is now occupied by 20 of our Marines. In the native gardens grow fruits such as bananas, mangoes, papayas, limes and coconuts. They grow all over the place and on Tulagi. We can pick one up and cut them open to drink the refreshing juice. Ivory nuts grow here too. I will collect some to show you when I get home.

I am decorating my buckskin jacket with native beads and sea shells I collect on the coral reefs. Also I'm writing the names of the islands I have been on out here such as Guadalcanal, Gavutu, Tulagi, etc. These are islands on which great history is being made.

I have two super buddies here who are Ed Fearon and Morris Baldwin who were sent up here with me from Noumea. Ed is from Santa Monica and was a life guard and great surfer and lady killer. Morris went to Stanford University and is of the famous Baldwin family of Maui in Hawaii. He has a beautiful wife and two children. He spends a lot of time looking at his wife's picture. We expect to have an exciting time here. It won't be too dull as we can watch the big Naval Battles from here out in Iron Bottom Sound. The Japs insist on throwing away their ships.

Oh yes, it's hot here but somehow heat never bothers me as I sweat so freely and I'm so lean and wiry. We have shows here too out on the old sports ground and surrounded by palm trees. I expect to see Navy doctor Hugh Patterson whenever his ship gets in here. He can get me some stamps from his ship's supply. He is one wild character. I'll send my letters to you at the family headquarters and you can pass them around to the sisters. It's going to rain again here any minute. Yup! Its starting now.

Please write as often as you can and send me stamps. I'll guarantee you exciting news as long as my letters don't mention where we are. I expect to be here for at least four to five months. Down in ComSoPac in Noumea they told us we would only have to be up here for about four months. Will see if they remember that promise. Well love and Merry Christmas

December 6th, 1942   CHASING BUTTERFLIES

When I wasn't on duty at the radio shack, I was chasing butterflies for an island insect collection. It was a terribly hot day and the butterflies luckily for them were eluding me. I did however catch a few from a net I'd made. I think the best time to go out after them is during the cool of early mornings. All the Marines I met along the way look at me askance as it must seem funny to them when they are faced with death in another battle they will be called upon to fight over on Guadalcanal. The Marines are still camped all over the island it seems. Lots of them live in tents near antiaircraft gun positions. It appears they still expect a big Jap invasion here which could come at any time. I am well armed with forty five and thirty eight revolvers and an Enfield British army rifle. I saw a huge old banyan tree where Marines had shot Jap snipers out of it.

December 7th, 1942.   BIG ANNIVERSARY OF THE BATTLE OF PEARL HARBOR

Just a year ago today the Japs had pulled off the lid on the world powder box and foolishly plunged us into World War II. But today they can no longer take us by surprise. We are all set for them but nothing developed. In the evening the Japs came down on the Tokyo Express but our PT boats gave them a good going over and the word is that our boats sank several of their transports. But as usual these overly optimistic reports by the gung ho P.T. boat skippers and crewmen are not usually confirmed. Yes, I am truly thankful to still be alive; and I hope I'm in the same condition a year from now.

December 8th, 1942   HOW BEAUTIFUL THE ISLANDS ARE

As hot and miserable as this island is it cannot be denied that it is very beautiful out here. Not so much on Tulagi which is badly shattered but as one looks out to other islands. The jungle is green as can be and the sea and mountains over at Guadalcanal are a wonder to behold in the late afternoons and early mornings. We have the loveliest sunsets and sun rises in all the world.

Most of the fellows in the BOQ are good guys. Soon I would have many good friends among the enlisted men who are the lucky survivors of the aircraft carried Hornet. These men were pulled out of the water before their ship went down. The Hornet was hit by submarines but was very stubborn and didn't want to sink. I tell about that battle soon in honor of my great radio gang who served on it.

I noted that the next recording on my Solomon Island Administration paper was dated December 25th, 1942. During those missing days in my diary writing I'd fallen sick with the deadly dengue fever. I was so sick and incapacitated that I didn't do any writing. I however, did have a vivid memory of what occurred during this time when my body was wracked with pain.

As I remember I was still sleeping in the Officers' washroom of the officers' mess house which had been partially bombed by us on August seventh invasion day. Dreamer Fearon, my good friend, sent up with me from Noumea, also had his cot here too. I think Ed was down with a bad case of Malaria. All the time I was on Tulagi I never got malaria; but the dengue fever was far more painful than malaria. I became so sick I could hardly move. The pain got into my bones. I just lay there on my cot in agony.

I remember that Captain O.O. Kessing, our Annapolis Base Commander would come into the room to wash, and he would look with pity on me lying on my cot when I couldn't even move. I don't remember if I tried to get into a fox hole when condition red alerted the base that Jap planes were overhead or on their way down to bomb us and especially at night when Washing Machine Charlie would make his usual runs. I was too stiff and sick to get up and into a fox hole as I just lay in bone-breaking agony.

We didn't yet have a base hospital, or at least I wasn't taken to one if there was one. The sickness was real bad for about a week. Then I slowly began to recover in about ten days time. Yet I was still too incapacitated to do duty in the radio shack. I remember I was allowed to take a picket boat over to Halavo Beach on Florida Island. I would go over for the day where I would visit the native village, get food at the PBY base there or at the PT Base up Hutchinson Creek sometimes. I would drink from coconuts, look for souvenirs, visit with natives and marines and Navy personnel. Just off where the water was deeper was a sunken Jap destroyer one could look down on. What a spooky sight it was as part of it was only a few yards down and the other end in deeper clear water. I would lay out on the warm sand and even got into the water to sooth the aches out of my body. I heard that lots of our G.I.s less lucky than I died of dengue fever transmitted by a mosquito.

December 21st, 1942   AFTERMATH OF DENGUE FEVER

I now backtrack a few days as I wrote again in my journal. The Navy still was putting out memorandums warning us not to write in diaries which the Japs might get a hold of and get useful information. However the Japs kept journals quite freely. We learned from them that their morale was very bad with lack of food, much sickness and troubles just like our poor Marines over on Guadalcanal. The Navy men on ships at least had plenty of food and a clean place to sleep. But when a Navy ship is hit by a Long lance Jap torpedo or by shell fire, all hell breaks loose and one can be dead in a hurry or swimming in oil and shark infested water. Luckily, many of our men in these battles could get rescued. The Japs were not usually so lucky as their surviving ships had to get back to their bases way up the line of Solomon islands.

I wrote freely in my diary as an uncensored letter to get by in case I was accused of keeping a diary against regulations. Here goes:

Dear Folks, Greetings to you and here is hoping I get some letters from you some day. That would be the best Christmas present I could possibly have. I hope Dad is O.K. I'm eager to know how he is. How is sister Marg making out? I sure wish I could help her with money for her college but as of now it is impossible for me to get any pay here.

Boy did I ever get laid low the other day with bursting headaches, fever and chills, and bone wracking pain. I felt so bad for a few days that all I could do was curse the war the Japs had brought on to us. We also out here take a very dim view of the G.I.s back in the States going to all the USO dances with the pretty girls and the draft dodgers. It was healthy to curse the government back home who appeared to us to be forgetting about us out here in the WAR. It seemed to be healthy to be bitching about something or other.

It is beautiful out here I had to admit in spite of any bitching I was doing about the war situation. But in the long run I could see that this was no place for a white American nor a black American. I think my attitude at this point was a result of having the dread Dengue fever. It took all the energy and ambition out of a person. I spent much of my free time over a map of the US planning where I'd go for future camping trips if I ever got out of here alive. I made up my mind to try to save my money. Once I fully recover from the bout of Dengue I resolved to get back my usual ambition.

This bloody war won't end too soon to suit me so I can get some of my life plans going once again. I want to be an explorer; and soon as I'm out of the Navy I'll plan a good expedition.

I now was trying to think of something cheerful. We luckily did have some good movies. I saw Jungle Book last night. There are a few super fellows here for friends so things could be much worse. We would make each other laugh by cursing things in general. I did have to admit that so far in the war I had been pretty lucky with some good duty there at Pearl Harbor and down in New Caledonia.

Gee, I'm down to my last airmail stamp—one for you folks at home and one for my imaginary girl friend, this Dorothy who I've never even dated and only imagine how nice she is. I could sure appreciate a nice snowy Christmas at home in northern Minnesota. The only thing that really keeps me going are my dreams of all the swell things I want to do when this bloody war is over. Right now I spend much time in the sack trying to recuperate from the Dengue fever. I will be O.K. in a few days. Once I get my canoe I hope to buy from the natives I'll be able to explore some of the islands nearby. I did get to a native village twice so far. I took pictures of a village over on Florida Island. All the natives were smoking cigarettes I'd passed out. Yes, everyone was smoking from grizzled old chiefs, little boys, and the women with their tremendous tits hanging down. Boy you would have laughed at me having a big council meeting and bartering with the people while trying to talk some pidgin English with them I learned a few of their native words as well. That really went over big with them. I seriously doubt if any of my photographs will turn out any good as the climate is too damp here for film.

I don't know how long I'll be out here? I don't imagine so terribly long as for one's health it is not any South Sea Island resort place. Sure will get happy when I get some good mail. Some good alcoholic beverages would sure cheer us up a bit. But the policy of the Navy seems to be, unlike the British Navy, that the home folks don't think the government should give us liquor. We do get a bottle of Australian beer once in awhile—ya, and sometimes with cigarette butts at the bottom of the bottles. Will try to write a more cheerful letter next time. Love from Tom of the South Seas

TULAGI RADIO STATION GANG
SURVIVORS OF THE CARRIER HORNET

This story was written by Thomas J. Larson and published by Mr. Ted Blahnik, the editor of the GUADALCANAL ECHOES.

Dear Ted,

I wish to pay tribute to my radio gang, the enlisted men who were survivors of the ill-fated carrier Hornet. These young men while riddled with malaria, dengue fever, fatigue, dysentery and other ailments, faithfully performed their skill as radio men and transmitter technicians. Many of the men were in the hospital, thus it was watch on watch off for those who could still stagger to the radio shack.

ADVANCED NAVAL BASE RINGBOLT

March 12, 1943

MEMO TO: Radio Officer, Ringbolt.

1. The following personnel is charged to the Radio Gang, Ringbolt

ANTHONY, Robert Paul	RM1c
BELROSE, David John	ARM2c
BOOTH, Charles Lester	RM2c
BRUNGARDT, Edward John	RM2c
BUCHANAN, Rally Fuller	RM1c
COX, John Joseph	RM3c
DANIELSON, Walden August	RM1c
DONAHOE, Charles Thomas Jr.	RM2c
* DOWD, Charles Arthur	RM2c
* ELLIS, Lloyd Wesley	RM1c
* FOREHAND, William Miles	RM1c
* FRENCH, Robert Eugene	RM2c
GOSE, John Newton	RM1c
GRANT, Harold Dean	RM2c
* HALE, Frank Mortimer	CRM(AA)
HASSELBACHER, Robert Charles	RM2c
HOLZMILLER, Adam (n)	RM1c
HUFF, James Loys	ARM2c
* JONES, Rufus Enloe	RM1c
KEOGH, James William	RM2c
LAVIN, John Joseph	RM2c
LETT, Fred Franklin	ARM2c
* MC CLURE, Lester Grant	CRM(AA)
MC KINNEY, Winfred Maurice	RM2c
* MERRITHEW, Robert Leslie	RM3c
MOTTOLA, Wesson Perry	RM3c
NORBERG, Boyd Fredrik	ARM2c
RAEMER, Harvey Daniel	ARM2c
SPLETTSTOSSER, Harry Roland	RM3c
TANNER, John Madden	ARM2c
TEVELDAHL, Gordon Elroy	ARM2c
WATSON, Ben Tillman, Jr.	RM2c
* WELCH, Donald Mansel	RM2c
* WHITE, Wilburn Glen	RM2c
ZDROJEWSKI, Leonard Francis	RM2c

RADIO TECHNICIANS:

FARR, James Ellsworth	RT2c
RAMBOW, Virgil Ralph	RT1c
RATHKE, Frank William	RT1c
UPTON, Keith Joseph	RT1c

RADIO MESSENGERS:

* MARTIN, Omar Leland	S1c
MC KENZIE, Donald Gordan	S1c

```
Radio - Communication:   Cont'd:

TELEPHONE OPERATORS:
        ERVIN, Hollis Edward            F1c
        MURPHY, James Oliver Jr.        F2c
        ~~PULVER, Richard Charles John~~  ~~F1c~~  TFD To SUPPLY

~~GUARD MAIL PETTY OFFICERS:~~
        ~~HUFF, Elwood Edward~~          QM2c
        ~~MOORE, Nolen Coston~~          Cox
```

  2. If there is any discrepency between this list and the personnel actually in the department please notify the Personnel Office immediately.

                                        W. Glenn Jones

To begin with, it was a typical example of the wartime Navy that I was to serve as a communicator a number of months at Tulagi. It was a paradox situation for I was brought up in the woods of northern Minnesota. I bought a Winchester 22 rifle for about five dollars when I was about ten years of age. I spent those glorious days of my early youth sneaking through the woods surrounding me, playing Indian, frontiersman, and hunter. I was a good candidate for leading Marine patrols through the jungle over at Guadalcanal. It so happened that while I was on a vagabond journey around the world from September of 1937 to May of 1939, after my first two years at the University of Minnesota, I had been a sailor on a tanker and on two freighters. The sea was in my blood so I joined the Navy. All went well in my Navy career after my ninety-day wonder DVG training at Northwestern University in Chicago. I became the Executive officer on YP 109, the beautiful two diesel 115 foot pleasure yacht of a lawyer by the name of Dempsey from Los Angeles. After a cruise out of Long Beach, California, and a stormy crossing in the Pacific, we arrived at the Section Base in Pearl Harbor on December 5th, 1941. My glorious dream of sailing around the Hawaiian Islands in YP 109 and pursuing lovely hula hula maidens on shore leave was shattered. At the Section Base I was given orders to report to CinCPac staff to be trained as a communicator. I didn't have the faintest idea what that involved; and knew little about radios. At the staff meeting at the CinCPac communication center, I was told to "Shut up, that's going to be your job in the Navy from now on."

Then I find myself in a Higgins Boat on November 30th, 1942 enroute to Tulagi from Guadalcanal to report to the flimsy radio shack for duty. And, to my surprise, before I knew it, I was to be in charge of Base communications because the head communicator is sick in hospital with malaria. For some strange reason I never got malaria while in the Solomons. Perhaps I was one of the most unorthodox reserve officers the U.S. Navy ever had. I had spent two years on my glorious vagabond journey on a "shoe string" and wasn't the least bit impressed with the many Navy regulations. I'd read an article by a Navy admiral saying regulations were necessary so that the stupidest fool could somehow blunder through to perform a job in the Navy.

I wish I could remember the names of all my wonderful radio gang. Radioman Forehand of Texas I got promoted to Chief. He also found some barbells so we could work out weight-lifting. Another young man was Jones who I promoted to Radioman First class. Hale from Alabama was most deserving, and he too was promoted to Chief. White of Nebraska made Radioman First. What a character was Ellis of Colorado whose ambition was to own a house of prostitution in Denver and keep all the women for himself he was so "loved starved". He too was promoted. In fact I got every man in the radio gang promoted. When the Executive Officer of the Base realized what I'd done, he blew his top. But it was too late for he had already signed the promotion papers. This fat cantankerous Annapolis officer had been sent to Tulagi for punishment for he as squadron commander of four destroyers ran onto a reef, and though it wasn't on his watch on the bridge he got the blame.

When condition red was ringing out and Washing Machine Charlie was dropping his bomb at random at night, the radio gang went off the air and we all headed for our fox hole under coconut logs. Then hurrah for the 26th CBies, These stalwart gentlemen blasted out a nice cave for us in the solid rock on a hillside so we could operate continuously. Lt. Tom Stoddard was indispensable as a skilled technician. He was in charge of the transmitters, and also the only one on Tulagi who could repair the electric coding machines which consistently needed repairs.

Another indispensable young man was Marine Private Hatfield of the infamous Hatfield clan of West Virginia who was our messenger. Hatfield, God Bless him, could make good brew out of prunes, raisins, apricots, pineapples—any fruit he could get his hands on. How gratifying it was to have Hatfield wake one up for duty in the middle of the night with a slug of his delicious and powerful brew from a jug he had found.

Well, one night a "duty struck" regular Navy Chief wanted to put a young North Carolina radioman on report for being too drunk to go on duty. "NO!" I claimed it would look bad on his record. "one of his buddies to take his watch."

Seaman Martin, who had been as far as fourth grade, was another messenger. He had been sick with malaria so many times that he was by this time really out of his mind and "rock happy." Captain Kessing, our Base Commander, took special delight in asking Martin how he should run the Base. Often poor delirious Martin volunteered this information without being asked. Radioman Merrithew almost died a number of times. It took a long time to convince our tyrant of an Executive officer to send poor Merrithew out on a hospital ship.

I will never forget the day when sailors and Marines were lining up to buy tobacco and pogey bait which was what candy was called. One of my radiomen, Norberg, a medium sized Norwegian-American from North Dakota, was in the line. He was a modest youth who was very quiet and reserved. A big tough-looking Marine insulted him by calling him a radio girl and attempted to push him out of the line. Then to the surprise of all, our radio girl systematically beat the big Marine to a bleeding pulp. It so happened that Norberg was a Golden Gloves boxing champion.

Then one day a young Ivy League Yale Reserve officer, who outranked me by several weeks, showed up. He was given my thankless job of head communication officer. What contempt he had for us old-timers and rock-happy radiomen and officers who would guzzle Hatfield's rock gut brew. We predicted that in about two weeks he would become depraved enough to join us. After all, the American Congress and public back home didn't think our fighting boys and men should be allowed to have regular liquor like the British. Well, our Ivy league "Hero" ended up in "hock" (confined to quarters) when the unfortunate young man failed to get an urgent message out to a submarine in time one dark night.

After eleven months of duty on Tulagi—Hell's Kitchen—I was quite rock happy myself and finally was reassigned as a liaison officer for temporary duty on HMNZS Leander, a New Zealand light cruiser which had been torpedoed in the bow in a battle in the Solomons.

Many of my wonderful radio gang enlisted men were sent up the line to another island in the Solomons. Shame! Radiomen were indispensable; Communication officers were not.

8

A Beachcomber on the Isle of Tulagi

December 25th, 1942.   CHRISTMAS DAY ON TULAGI

Today it is supposed to be Christmas. I can honestly say I don't really want to have another one like this one. Christmas on this lousy wrecked island of Tulagi with all its heat and disease does not get a high bounce on the many islands I've visited. This is my fourth Christmas away from home. There was one in Pasadena, California, in 1937, the next one in 1938 was in Tunis, North Africa, then at Pearl Harbor in 1941, and now here. I have just recovered from bone-wracking Dengue Fever and it didn't make me like the war and the Navy all that much. I'm just living now for the day I'm out of the military and on an expedition of my own. I've known since I was two years old that yes, I would be an explorer and making up my own rules.

Luckily I got the first mail I've received for two months. I got letters from two sisters: Marjorie, who wants money from me for college, and Barbara. Now that I'm on the best payroll I've ever had, I will be glad to help out my sisters until they can get good jobs to help out the war effort.

Actually how lucky could us guys out here be. We had pretty good Christmas chow with turkey, olives, celery, potatoes, peas and plum pudding. We also were issued a bottle of beer and a carton of cigarettes. Ed Fearon went over to Guadalcanal to see if he could find any mail for us. Haven't seen him since. I did also get some letters from gals in the States. It is very nice of them to write. Wish I could do them some good.

Saw a good show called *Secret Jap Agent*. A beautiful girl drives me crazy as I want to get my hands on one so much. Also saw the show *Sundown* with the beautiful woman Jean Tierney in it. She is one luscious beautiful creature. When I get home, I'm going to date plenty of those divine creatures. Yes, I promise myself that resolution. I get a big kick out of the five pups from native dogs who play around while the show is going on. Also the Protestant Chaplin is a regular Holy Roller religion monger. He doesn't inspire much religion feeling in me. I get religious when Washing Machine Charlie is overhead and I'm in a fox hole. Its quite true there are no atheists in fox holes. The new Captain Kessing is kicking friend Morris Baldwin out of the washroom like Ed Fearon and I. That means all my pictures of those sexy woman like Jane Russell and Rita Hayworth will have to come down. We were moved up to the side of a hill into an army tent. Baldy is of the famous missionary Baldwin family who took over Maui who gave the Hawaiians the Bible in exchange for their land. He went to Stanford and is madly in love with his beautiful wife.

December 27th, 1942.   LIFE ON TULAGI

Letter home: The flies are terrible. They crawl over everything. I have to wear a helmet and a shirt to keep the filthy things out of my hair and body. It's a wonder we are not all dead from typhoid fever and dysentery. The Navy has filled us so full of vaccination shots that we should be immune to every disease. We are not though. About one third of the men on the base are down with a fever all the time. Poor Ed Fearon has the malaria again. I hope I don't get it. So far I've been lucky though I had dengue fever which is much more painful. I however have pretty much recovered from the dengue and feel pretty good. When one is sick out here it sure makes one hate this war.

I'm on watch now with the radio gang. They are all swell. I wish all the officers could be as good all around fellows as the enlisted men. Some of the officers stationed here are real bastards—especially our Executive officer Commander J who was sent up here because his destroyer ran into a coral reef. He was in command of a squadron of three or four destroyers. I heard later he wasn't on watch when it happened but he being in command had to take the blame. He was sent up here as punishment. He is an Annapolis officer. He likes to take out his anger on us reserve officers. He is a short and fat mean-spirited character. We really despise him. Luckily I was able to keep clear of his wrath.

I spent some time today reading *Readers Digest*, and washing clothes. I was lucky enough to buy five air mail stamps which are so scarce out here. The show this day was *Escape* with that most beautiful and adorable actress Norma Shearer. I would give anything to have a chance to love such a gorgeous woman. I'd seen the show before but that didn't matter. I'd go to see it ten times just to imagine I was loving such a woman.

You should see my beard and moustache. I'll cut it off the day I leave this hell hole island. Gee! I'd do anything to get to the States even for a few days. You can't imagine how wonderful that would be. I think I might get paid pretty soon. Then I will send Marjorie $100 to help out with expenses at college. Love, Tom

December 29th, 1942. THE DAILY BEACHCOMBER

I stood watch four to eight this morning. I am still a little weak from having had the dengue fever but I'm getting better. After my watch I rested awhile then emptied out my gas mask bag and put in my diving face plate glasses and some tobacco for trading with the natives. Then I got a ride over to Halavo native village where the Naval air station is. There I saw old chief Patrick and some of his tribesmen. Most of them were women. One was a pretty girl just sprouting breasts and several older women were very well slung with razor-strap breasts from nursing children so long. One poor woman had horrible yaws and carried a baby. The baby had bad yaws also. An Englishman in the camp was treating this affliction. The festering sore had myriads of flies in them. I heard this yaws could be cured with penicillin.

I then walked up the beach a bit. On the way I crossed a tiny brook. There I saw climbing fish that appeared to be amphibious for it swims through the water then swiftly darts over land and on the surface of the water.

I put on my face plate and ventured out on the shallow coral reef. A beautiful fairy land was under and all around me. Fantastically beautiful colored fish swam around me and were quite unafraid. Tiny fish peered out at me from every crevice in the coral. One fat clumsy looking fish with great goggle eyes got under an archway and stared at me quite stupidly and sleepily. I swam around him in a threatening manner but that didn't seem to disturb him in the least. I then saw some sea horses who swam along in a vertical position and were always just out of my reach. Then I saw a huge star fish. One kind had cream colored skin with big red warts on it. Another one was blue. The sea lilies were exquisite and beautiful delicate forms which weaved most gracefully with the underwater currents. Long appendaged brittle stars intertwined their ugly bodies around and through the coral. Tiny sea anenomies pulled their forms into the coral as I passed. Clams of brilliant blue and green snapped shut when I came near. I saw several types of sea cucumbers and many fascinating forms of coral. The sea was teeming with beautiful life. A tiny jelly fish pumped by me but did not escape being captured for several moments. On my delightful journey of exploration I was now to encounter live sponges. Though I never tired of my new discoveries, the sun was becoming dangerously hot. I headed once more along the beach.

At a Navy camp I was invited to partake of food with the men and to "shoot the bull" with them. They generously gave me some powerful alcoholic brew they had concocted. Their commanding officer had ordered them to throw away the deadly poison as an officer had nearly died from drinking it. It gave me only a mild stomach ache for I had a cast-iron stomach.

Chief Patrick of the local Solomon Islanders gave me a delicious coconut drink. One of his tribesmen climbed a coconut tree in record time and cut down a whole cluster of nuts with a machete. He had tied his ankles together with a fiber and worked his way up the slender trunk of the tree like a measuring worm. To separate the thick green husk from the inner nut a sharp stake was driven into the ground. The husk was peeled off by slamming the nut down on the sharp stake then tearing pieces off.

After observing the dehusking operation, I made a deal with Chief Patrick for the purchase of a native alligator canoe sometime later "manana" as they would say. My day on Florida Island at Halavo came to a happy and successful conclusion. War had some happy days.

On my way home to Tulagi the Higgens boat passed over the sunken Jap destroyer. Its ghostly form lay like a huge dead monster in the clear water. I could see the guns, stack, torpedo tubes, and the bridge. I thought what a most welcome sight it could be if the whole Jap fleet could be seen down under the water.

9

The Glorious Year of 1943 Starts Off With A Bang

January 1st.   THE YEAR OF OUR LORD 1943 'tis said.

The new year for this great World War II started off with a BANG! I was just coming off watch and walking along the sea wall when a lot of pistol and rifle shots rang out. I thought it was some kind of an encounter until I remembered it was the New Year. I heard shouts out on the ships and around the harbor. I added mine to all the others. Mine were the weirdest of all with my Indian war whoops, loon calls and owl calls of northern Minnesota. I slept awhile then was up at seven to take part in the most interesting expedition I had experienced in the Solomons.

A half dozen officers and two seamen and with a Higgins boat was what would make up our trip. Lets see-there was Lt. Commander Wahl, Lt. Grace (of the Grace Lines family), Ensign Greenough a supply officer, Lt. Graton, Ensign Rosenberg of New Orleans and was a supply officer, Loftus and 1. We had a good supply of corned meat to trade with the natives and two enlisted natives who were attached to the American Marines as scouts. Two sailors ran the boat while the rest of us basked in the hot sun.

We followed a channel marked by wooden buoys between Tulagi and Florida islands. My eyes were wide open for everything and everywhere I looked was delightful to the eyes of a romanticist as me. We followed the coast of Florida Island northward. The shoreline was a jungle paradise with beautiful palms fringing white sand beaches while higher up on the hillsides grew the trees of the dense tropical jungle. In a few places the barren outcropping rocks could support only grass. These grasses in patches blended beautifully with the surrounding jungle. We saw cliffs of limestone made up of the bodies of diatoms and minute animal bodies. Countless caves carved by the wind and sea indented these limestone cliffs. It was a wonderful sight to see the green jungles, the meadows, the tall palms, sand beaches and cliffs, and the sea of many colors. We could look off to our left and see historic Guadalcanal and Savo Islands. Off Savo billions of dollars of ships of the Japanese, United States, and the Australian navies lie useless on the bottom of the sea, Even now we were daring to venture out in a defenseless Higgins boat. We have only three 45 pistols as anti-aircraft, submarine, and surface ship defense and also for landing parties.

The sea was full of life visible to us explorers. We saw many porpoises, flying fish, and countless bright colored fish in the shallow water. We passed several native villages. One village was in a picturesque little bay. Nicholas, the Native marine scout, guided us into the bay where we drifted while he made a trip ashore to the village in an alligator-shaped wooden canoe. I could see the brilliantly colored coral bottom through the transparent blue water. This sight, regardless of any danger from sharks was too much for me. My clothes were quickly off my body and I was over the side with my face plate diving glasses. I swam down in the wonderful clear water to rise again and again plunge into the realm of the Solomon seas, home of sunken ships and monsters of the deep. A large blue unwilling starfish was brought to the surface. The coral was too tough to break off with the hands so remained where nature meant that it should remain. Loftus and Graton soon followed me into the water. It was one of the most delightful swims I had ever experienced.

Nicholas came back and we continued on up along the coast toward Japan. We came to the end of Number One island of Florida, and crossed a half mile strait up to Number Two Florida Island and there saw two fair sized native villages. We landed in a bay at the beautiful village of Olevuga. We were greeted by a score or more of men and little black kids. We shook hands with everyone, then left Nicholas to handle everything. This was his home town. Here lay one of the most beautiful and peaceful native villages I'd ever seen. I didn't miss much in my inspection especially the women who were naked except for short bright-colored skirts. But I will go into that later. I noticed the intricate construction of the houses made of bamboo and interwoven palm leaves. The spears and kitchen utensils and the alligator canoes were interesting. The canoes had the alligator tail going up and the front of the canoe was the head of the reptile all beautifully inlaid with mother of pearl. The timbers of the canoe were glued together with a resin. They had tapa cloth mats and beautiful gardens. Huge banyan trees and bamboo grew in the village, soft carpets of grass grew beneath these trees.

The natives now brought us presents of bananas, pineapples, coconuts, papayas, and beads, wooden cups, canes, grass skirts. We gave them tinned meat in exchange.

Now for a description of the people. The kids were for the most part naked. I noticed lots of ugly yaws and sores on the people. The women were quite a sight for sore eyes. Huge firm teats stuck out from the young women like shelves. It was all I could do to refrain from reaching out and grabbing these tremendous things to see if they were the real thing. But what a sight! Some of the girls would have made Jane Russell blush as far as size went. At the next village we saw the same sights, great quantities of bosoms of the ladies, of course, and little suckling babies and kids of all sizes. We saw a native church here. The native preacher put his white clothes on for us and his cross. Then he took us through his church. It was church of England. Simple hand cut planks made the seats. There was a simple altar and Bible which had been translated into the native language. The church was decorated with palm leaves and was very beautiful and simple.

These natives are very religious and law abiding. We were given more fruit here and we in return gave them meat. Loftus took some pictures. I unfortunately had left my camera back at the base as I was afraid of it being discovered and taken away from me. Too bad! We had been warned not to take pictures by the authorities. I was determined to come back here again.

I went swimming several more times, then we had to shove off. As we left, the simple and happy natives sang us some church hymns. Though they couldn't read music, they had wonderful harmony and sincerity.

For two hours under the blistering hot sun and heat we cruised through the blue enchanting water. These waters held the bodies of thousands of fighting men—needless dead to the greed and folly of wretched mankind and the war gods. It was hard to believe that such beauty could be associated with this horrible damned needless war of which by force I am part of it all-yes, and very indifferently.

January 4th, 1943   THE WAR HEATS UP

It was a cool and lovely day for this Hell's Kitchen place in the South Seas. I always enjoy the beauty of these islands, the dreaded Solomons. I had the morning watch so was off at 12. On my rock on the hill above I took a sun bath and a good look around over the island and the sea. A Little New Zealand minesweeper sank a Japanese submarine out there the other day. It was a sub that was twice as big as the minesweeper with bigger guns and more men. They rammed her, then shot her full of holes, depth charged her. When she came up, they gave it to her again.

As I sat on my rock lookout the guns began to bark out from all over the place. The trigger-happy and mad Marines were just practicing shooting. Ed Fearon,

Baldy, and I were going to start moving but then this idea soon petered out for the time being.

So Ensign Greenough, a scruffy lad, but a great guy, and I went on an expedition in his dugout canoe. We ditched our clothes and got in the tiny dugout and paddled with our hands around Tulagi to a tiny island out in the channel about 100 yards from shore. We had to bail out several times in shallow water. I ran around the island bare naked and bare-footed through the dense undergrowth. It was then I heard a heavy body crashing through the jungle growth. It was too heavy for a lizard and about the right size for a small crocodile they have here. The coral was tough on my feet so I headed for the water. My diving glasses worked swell. I saw some rare looking animals and beautiful sea lilies. Then I climbed a rock off the island. A swift flow of water rushed between the island and the rock and out to a coral reef. After exploring the bottom of the sea, we paddled to shore and walked around to where our clothes were. Then we walked through the CB camp without a stitch of clothing on, with hibiscus flowers in our hair. We got some chow down in the enlisted mens' mess hall. There we got far better food than the officers got, with real butter.

When I was about to go to bed, I got word of an impending battle out at sea here. I got Dreamer Fearon out of bed and we climbed way up to a gun position high on a hill. Then we saw lots of search lights and anti-aircraft fire over on Guadalcanal. We saw flares later on over by Savo. The word was that twenty Jap destroyers were coming down the slot. Our dive bombers were supposed to attack them but the stupid bastards fouled up. They foolishly flew over Henderson Field with the search lights over them, then had orders to get the hell out of there. The Navy planes had dropped their flares and spotted numerous Jap destroyers. The damned Army planes kept calling "Where are the Jap ships?' "Where are the ships?" They were putting on a big dumb act miles away from where they should have been. The bright flares were plainly visible to us way over here—still the planes up in the air claimed they couldn't see them. Finally, when the flares had burned out and the Jap destroyer had escaped, the torpedo planes got out where they were supposed to make their attack. It was too late now. They cussed out the Navy fliers who had done their part of the job. Finally in despair and disgust, they were called in to land at Henderson Field. This is one of the examples of how we are winning the war in the Solomons. Just one mind you.

January 14th, 1943.   FINALLY GETTING SOME OF OUR PAY

I missed quite a few days here from my last writing in my diary—the DAILY BEACHCOMBER. It really rained—just poured down in great buckets, We wallowed in mud. In the afternoon Dreamer, Baldy, and I got a ride to the Alchiba ship on a most important issue. We wanted to get some of our long overdue pay. The paymaster of the ship opened our accounts for us then closed them forthwith. I got $25. And a $100 check for my sister Marjorie and $75 a month allotment for the First National Bank of Brainerd. So I've gotten it lined up so I will save $125 a month. While our accounts were being worked on we were in the wardroom listening to phonograph records and looking at magazines. We shot the breeze with Ensign Pulver and Fennon for awhile, then I went on the 20–24 evening watch.

As the name Pulver came up I will tell about him. This character was an Annapolis graduate but most untypical. He had the dirtiest warped mind of any young Navy officer I'd ever encountered. But he was a good guy The Base Commander wanted to have his commission taken away from him because of his filthy language. What a joker this Pulver.

Well, when I was on duty, we suddenly got CONDITION RED—then all of a sudden we heard our anti-aircraft guns blazing away and a plane was flying overhead. Everyone grabbed for his light and was out the door of the flimsy radio wooden shack. I headed up to the edge of the cliff and looked around like a fool while the guns were going off. This was the first excitement for some time—ya, since last night. Nothing happened except for shooting two of our own Marines, so we put on the lights in the radio shack and went back to work again.

January 15th, 1943   RAIN AND HEAT

Dreamer Fearon and I rolled out of our sleep for chow at the Captain's private establishment. We stomped up then back to camp. It was steaming hot today. After a week of tropical downpours and now sunshine, the air was very humid and hot as a boiler. Our green camouflaged tent we'd been moved into adsorbed all the heat. I melted. We had to put away our precious pictures to keep them from getting water soaked and ruined. I split a big papaya and the Dreamer and I demolished the delicious thing in record time. It was from a nearby shade papaya tree which grew close to our tent. Our tent was near the edge of a hill with our fox hole down in front. It had big tough coconut logs over it. Most comforting to have a fox hole so close.

We ran a smooth watch and then got to go on a ship. The officer of the deck was Lutz, a Swede from Minnesota, so all was well. He gave us four magazines. Dreamer and Pops Baldy came aboard so we got a few little things from the ship's service. It sure was fun to be able to spend a little money. By candle light, Dreamer and I composed letters to a couple of girls in the States, our favorites.

Harper, a New Zealand pilot, told us how he brought in the heavy cruisers of the November 1st battle. His description of what he saw was a bloody story—how men were killed by concussion, burned to death at their battle stations, bodies scattered over the bulkheads, poor survivors in the oil-covered water. It was terrible and I want none of it EVER! I then dreamed—forgot the war, and imagined how Dorothy, this beautiful young girl back in my home town and I would have hot love for each other.

Actually this Harper character was an Australian. He had his tent next to ours. He was a crusty tough old planter who had been in these islands for a long time. He knew where the coral reefs were and thus was most indispensable to our Navy in bringing in ships from these dreadful night battles. He was tattooed heavily, was rather bow-legged, and a most delightful character who I will tell more about later. We did hear lots of good war stories from him.

January 24th, 1943   BEING THE ASSISTANT COMMUNICATION OFFICER

This day to satisfy Naval Regulations out here about not keeping a journal, I addressed a letter to my sister Barbara I never sent. It goes as follows: "Sure was swell getting your wonderful letter. You are one swell girl and I love you alot. Of all my sisters, you are the one that it is the easiest to get along with.

You would laugh at me now. I'm sitting bare assed naked on a rock in the hot tropical sun high over the island. Excitement and history is in the making all around me. Lots of people all over but not a woman on the island or within miles—white women that is, I mean of course. Will tell you about the native women later.

Boy am I sweating here! But I love it and am getting a tan and big muscles from exercising. One of my radiomen, I think Forehand from Texas, got some barbells for us to workout on. Also he and others tied a thick line (rope) up around a tree limb. I am good at rope climbing and that really puts on muscle in arms and shoulders.

Gee, Barbs, no matter how bad a place is I soon adapt myself and always manage to enjoy life. Boy what a view I have here. I heard that Bob Olson of Aitkin is over on the next island. Will have to try to find him. Its going to storm here pretty soon. And the rains here come every day in these South Sea islands. See some most majestic sunsets over the sea and the "Islands of No Return" for the Japs. It isn't a very popular place for them.

Saw a wonderful show the other night. It was *"Song of the Islands"* with Betty Grable. It was all about Hawaii. I plan to roam all over the Hawaiian Islands when the war is over. They are so beautiful.

Am now quite happy here. I wasn't when I had the Dengue Fever. I have a tent where I live with my best pal Dreamer Fearon of Santa Monica. He is a wonderful surfer and is as lazy and happy-go-lucky as me. He likes to travel and loaf. He loves wild parties and beach life. We really get along.

I'm Assistant Communication officer so run things the easy going way I like best. I have a swell gang of radio men to work with. For fun we go to shows, visit ships, bull session, and make plans for when the war is over and if we get to go to Wellington and Sydney.

I dove for some Jap souvenirs in the water the other day. It is wonderful swimming here in the coral reefs regardless of the sharks. I find plenty of things to do here—adventures etc.. It is interesting and fun to visit native villages. The natives run around almost naked. The women wear grass skirts and have tremendous tits, and do most of the work and are quite ugly. I will bring back some native souvenirs.

Must quit now as the sun is too hot—one burns rapidly. Orchids are growing all around here.

There are such beautiful flowers all around here. Well, so long for now, Tom.

10

Life on Tulagi as the War Goes on

January 25th, 1942   **ADAPTING TO ISLAND LIFE IN WARTIME**

I exist, but little more, as the days pass on. Each day I become lazier and more indifferent to the world around me. When a man becomes this way, it is time for him to awaken himself as best he may. I spend most of my time planning and dreaming of the future when this war is over. I write a few letters, stand my communication watches, eat, sleep, occasionally walk way around to Blue Beach, and to a show. I exercise every other day. Outside of that I do practically nothing. So I realize it is high time for me to awaken for there are things to be done small though they may be.

Today perhaps has been my laziest of all days. I lay around all morning and continued to do nothing all afternoon until I went on watch where I did as little as possible. I must awaken and be true to my adventure-loving soul. So, I will awaken, hot though the days may be. If I will look around, grit my teeth, and act I'm sure I can find much to do. I will read from the limited supply of books on hand. I will get inspired as best I can and write my book, I will get a canoe and explore Florida Island. I will collect insects and relics. I will exercise religiously. I must have a faithful diary and accounts of war stories, and tall tales from the Marines. If a man opens his eyes there is so much to do, so much of interest here. I will write letters to all whom letters are due. I must arise and act quickly while the time slips by. Some day I will be leaving here to better or worse places.

I write by the dim light of an oil lamp in this Solomon Island. Men of the Construction Battalion work below me widening a road which goes through a rock ridge. They work night and day. These men are professional men who worked in Texas oil fields and really know how to do work much better and faster than the Navy way. The war goes on as usual. Time drags on and I have only a mild interest in the war. All I care about is that it will soon be over with. There are wild rumors of a coming Jap attack. Let them come and they will never want to come here again. We have six carriers, six super battleships, and hundreds of planes to maul them to death. Big operations must be pending. The Japs will have their day and soon. Germany is on the retreat in Africa and Russia. The Japs are stalemated and slowly giving ground. Bloody battles are being fought across the way on Guadalcanal. I will have to get some of the latest stories. I hear that over 1,000 Japs were killed the other day by our brave Marines and Army. The 164th North Dakota-Minnesota Army Division are doing great with their brand new rifles and experience in hunting back home.

We blasted hell out of them at Munda and gave them a bad time. We had condition red here almost every night. Baldy has had a fox hole dug for us so we are all set for the big day that the Japs decide to drop bombs on us here. It is wonderful to see our big B-17s and new P-38s fly over to give the Japs a very bad time up the line in the Solomons like New Georgia.

Ed just brought in a couple of oranges he swiped off a ship. These are the first oranges we have seen for many months. It is comfortable here at night. It is usually bull session when I should be writing tonight. Its beautiful moonlight tonight. so we might expect Washing Machine Charley down. Life goes on—its one big camping trip and no sea duty. I'll take camping any day. A rock can't be sunk like a ship. Already life has picked up since I have written this much. Our desk is just covered with pictures of beautiful women in various tantalizing positions and dress (undress). Dorothy's picture dominates my hopes for great return and imagined hot romance. What a fool I was to imagine these kind of things from a young girl I'd never dated.

January 26th, 1943.   GUNS GOING OFF

At four in the morning I unconsciously became aware of something alarming. I heard dull and rapid five inch gun blasts. This kept up continuously so I yelled to Ed and Baldy to get up. All three of us tumbled out of our sacks and jumped into our fox hole under the coconut logs. I was bare naked until I decided to put on my shoes and poncho. The guns were really booming. Some of our destroyers were shooting at Jap planes. Later these planes came over Tulagi and gave us a big thrill. No bombs were dropped but it could happen any night now. Finally dozed off and forgot about the Jap planes.

In the morning I sat in the tent and sewed beads on my buckskin jacket. I have a beautiful design of pikaki beads. Also every morning I pull dead lizards out from under my mattress. It stinks here too. I think dead Japs must be buried underneath our tent.

Ed and I went on watch with flowers over our ears, and shirts off and in general very much beach comber types. Had a big time on watch with the radiomen, and did actually break a few messages on our electric coding machines.

Had a workout with Ed on the barbells. We were toning up good—I feel 100 percent better. The rope climbing is really good exercise. I could do it at least five times climbing up about 15 feet.

We expect big things to happen tonight. Working in the coding shack lets us read the messages about expected events. Planes from a Jap carrier attacked Guadalcanal. I don't know how the battle came out? A Jap task force is headed this way we think. Big days are ahead of us. It should be our big chance to screw up the Japs. It is thundering now—a big storm is ahead—it is cooling us at any rate. Ed and I are going out to look for spare chow tomorrow.

January 27th, 1943.   OUR LIFE ON TULAGI

I slept through a Condition Red. The old Jap planes came over again. The only time the stinking yellow bellies dare come our way is at night. They haven't dropped any bombs on us yet. We have no decent warning system here at all. Down at the dock below a bell is rung a few times which no one can hear.

I had the 8 to 12 watch. Dreamer and I. While Dreamer was out collecting spare chow such as cans of pineapple juice, apple sauce, peaches etc. I did the gory decoding. The radio gang boys were hauling palm logs for our bomb shelter so I gave them a hand. They are a swell bunch of good lads. After my watch Baldy and Ed were fooling around with a big barrel of water while I sewed beads on my buckskin jacket. When the big fruit boat came in from Florida Island we scrambled down and loaded up with bananas, papayas and pineapples. We were going to make some potent brew from papaya juice. It sure looks good by our tent with a big bunch of bananas hanging up in the old banyan tree.

We visited Captain Larson of the Marine Corps. His home is in Brookings, South Dakota. He said the 147th Field Artillery of South Dakota is coming out. My distant cousin on my mother's side of the family, Col. Foster, might be with them. If he is, I will make some official visits with him and his troops.

We are sitting in our tent now in the quiet of evening before the guns and bombs of the later evening disturb our sleep. I never worry much though. I'm either going to get it or not. I just hope not.

January 29th, 1943.   BUILDING UP THE MUSCLES

I visited with Dr. Kingston of Bemidji, Minnesota. We had a long and interesting visit. He is working on malaria control and was a medical school classmate of

Dr. Petroberg of my home town of Aitkin. He is a swell guy. I now plan to go down to study his books and learn about malaria. I just don't want to get the damned sickness which is laying so many of our troops low.

In the afternoon I crapped out. It is awfully hot and sultry. It takes all the strength out of a fellow. It was my weight-lifting day so I finally got off my duff and went down to the outdoor gym with Dreamer Fearon. I really am progressing fast. I have advanced on the average of 15 pounds on each weight exercise. I really felt good by the time I was through. I haven't gained much weight but have become considerably stronger.

I made a stem for my Indian peace pipe. I burned a hole through the wooden stem with a red hot wire. Had nothing but lots of work to do on the evening watch.

January 30th, 1943.   MEETING PEOPLE AND MR. LIZARD

I slept until 9:30 and did I ever enjoy my sack. Finally I got up to take a sun bath and looking for my reptile friend, a white spotted two foot long lizard who lives in the cliff above us. I had the afternoon watch when I had my first trouble with one of my radio men. This fellow, a Chief, is a regular and a little duty struck. He goes by stupid Navy regulations and thinks he is too good to do certain things. He likes to put some of our boys on report as well which I claim doesn't look good on their record.

When I got, down to my tent from watch, I found a nice cane and a Solomon war club on my bunk given to me by my Native police friend Salama. They are both beautiful pieces of local hard wood and make great souvenirs. I really have some local arts and crafts to show for myself for my collection. After chow Dreamer and I got in a boat and went out to the ship Carina to see Eggerman who was on our staff of ComSoPac down in Noumea. We climbed aboard and found our friend. We shot the bull for awhile, then we got a condition red for a few minutes. A big Lt. came and sat down by us. His name was Herbert Michels who went to the University of California at Berkeley. He was a friend of Jim Orr and was a shot put record holder of the West Coast and was to be on the American team in the next Olympics. He was one swell fellow. I had remembered seeing him working out in the gym at Cal. We went down in the wardroom and had coffee and had a big time. It sure is fun to visit these ships. We rode back in a Higgins boat with a lot of native laborers.

January 31st, 1943   TRYING TO KEEP HEALTHY

I am taking life easy—eating plenty and building up reserve strength to ward off malaria—for that is the only way to live in the tropics. I sure like the boys, the survivors of the Aircraft carrier Hornet, who are my radio gang. I try to keep them all in good spirits. Eventually I got most of them promoted before the mean old Executive Officer got wind of what I was up to. I have been thinking alot lately as to just how I can best spend my spare time. I do feel good now. I'm in good health and have my old fighting drive back. While this feeling lasts I wish to do something. I believe a man should recognize his opportunities. The opportunities I see which I have here in these dreaded Solomon islands are a good chance to read up on the available literature I haven't read for years. I plan to write up my travel experiences, collect local insects, and souvenirs of native artifacts. My main ambition and hope is that I can keep healthy and strong

Subject: **Florida Island Native language Words**   (Date) by Tom Larson Dec. 1942

liangu na ulelambu – I catch butterfly
uto – beautiful
bola – bird
kula – friend
hogogu – brother
vavinegu – sister
tomagu – my father
tinagu – my mother
na niu – coconut
na vudi – banana
na vali – house
na beti – water
na tahi – salt water
na pari – ground
na vatu – stone
na gai sule – big tree
na gai pile – small tree
na gau – knife
na posu – axe
na kudo – hen
na kokoroko – rooster
na bua – bitternut
na kura – leaf
na poke – line (fish)
na ubi – yam
na pana – (a fruit)
na gole – cabbage
na kavakava – comb
na tiro – glasses
na kirisa – small basket

mua liogu – I don't want to
to eliogu – yes I want to
TONATUAINAU – I GO NOW
INAU I AM
IGOE – YOU ARE
NA TUA LEG
NA LIMA ARM
NA GINHIRI – FINGER
NA GUGU NAIL
NA ULU HEAD
NA KULI EAR
NA MANA MOUTH
NA GIDU LIPS
NA LIVO – TEETH
NA THU NOSE
NA MATA EYE
NA NARA FACE
SOPAU SIT DOWN
NA SUSU TIT
TUGURU STAND
NA SAND
NA SIMU STAR
NA VULA MOON
NA PARAKO CLOUD
NA KOLA MANGO
NA VAKA SULE BIG SHIP
NA VAKA PILE SMALL SHIP
KAIKOLI LAY DOWN
KATONA WE GO
EMUALIAGU TO NOT WANT TO
NA KEKEVE BEAD
AGE HELLO
TAUGU MY WIFE
TAUMU YOUR WIFE
DALEGU MM BEGINNING
XXXXX
DALEMU YOUR BEGINNING
EL YES
TAHO NO
NATAVU SUGAR CANE
MXXBRRX MATURU SLEEP
RARAI WORK
SAMA RISES RUNS
BEI SAMA NO RUN
SOKA TUA FINISH

Poor Ed is now plenty sick with malaria. Poor kid he is quite depressed and pathetic with ulcers in his stomach as he is a hot tempered Irishman. I saw a movie about numerous beaches in the States. What a wonderful sight. I can hardly wait until I get back to some of those glorious beaches. I helped swipe some corned beef from an abandoned Marine Camp. We intend to trade with the natives tomorrow for souvenirs.

This winds up my life and adventures for the month of January of a most momentous month in these war torn islands.

11

The War Drags on

February 2nd, 1943.   EXPLORING AROUND ON TULAGI

There was a big sea battle out here last night up around Savo island. From the coast watchers up the line in the Solomons we had heard that 19 Jap destroyers were headed down the slot. So our PT boats were sent out to harry them a bit. I wish the big shot admirals down in Noumea would get off their asses and stop the Japs from all their mischief down this way. But then the longer the war goes on the more rich people there will be in the States—ya, making war so they can get richer. And lots of the big shot's kids that go to Ivy league universities are draft dodgers. Or, if they do get out here their congressmen get them out soon.

Well, as I was going to say—we lose several PT boats and the Japs lose about three destroyers. They lost some in a mine field we had just laid to catch them. We came out on top in that engagement, but it is sure taking us enough time to take one island over there in Guadalcanal. The boys are really cleaning up though on the Canal. The Japs are pulling back, running out of food and other supplies, and are very sick too.

Ed and I went on an expedition after dinner. We located a nice hill up above us where we intend to go to when we want privacy and to keep away from the dreaded officers, quarters and the holy terror of Tulagi, that Exec Officer J of the Naval Academy. Ed found a Springfield rifle he is going to fix up. We followed the ridge which went through lots of rocks. The jungle was full of small animal life, mostly insects and lizards. We left the jungle and followed the coast. The army has moved in to take the place of the battle worn Marines. We saw some lonely graves of Marines who died for the God of war and hatred. We also saw the land fish who scamper over the land and water. These are lung fish of some species. Had a swell swim then crawled out on a log past a wooden fence and barbed wire entanglements. Had to splash through water and mud as the trail was at the foot of a cliff and the sea really pretty high.

I forgot just what day it was, but one day when Ed and I were way up at the end of the island, we got out on a coral reef where I found many small beautiful money live cowry shells. I collected them and put them out where the ants could clean them out. This gave me a great collection. Some I sewed onto my buckskin jacket.

We resolved to get off our asses and really get out and do some exploring while we are here. Saw some real isolated camps back in the jungle. There is plenty to do. There are too many malaria mosquitoes here for living a healthy life. We take atabrine which turns us a yellow color. I plan to get over to Florida Island and to really do some good exploring. I must somehow get a native canoe.

February 21st, 1943. THE HEAD COM OFFICER GETS NASTY

I have laid off writing in my diary for some time. Too bad. I will tell you why. Old man Wall made me assistant communication officer, and made the big mistake of getting nasty to me one day. I couldn't hit him like I wanted to but I sure felt like it. He lost his temper and being so dumb and bull headed he did all the talking. I should have given him some good back talk. However I wisely kept my mouth shut. Also I should have given up my job as assistant com officer. I didn't want it anyway. The old nasty bastard is now going to get MY famous SILENCE TREATMENT. I won't talk to him nor visit him in the hospital when he got malaria. I will just ignore him and no longer speak to him nor visit him in the hospital. He soon got shipped out; and it was good riddance of the nasty bastard.

Well, Dreamer is now doing all the getting around while old Wolf Larson, the so-called Horrible Swede, has to put in much time at the radio shack with my new position as Assistant Communication Officer. I did manage to get away quite often to read books. I'm reading Zane Grey's and Jack London's books. I get so enthusiastic after reading these great books that I forget about the war, the heat and anything unpleasant about my environment. I read of the places I love and it makes me very happy. I spend much time also exercising with the barbells. The results are good for I have put on muscle on my arms, shoulders, neck and chest. Reading and exercising are my two main passions. Some of the boys are getting out of here so there is hope. I'm sure I'll get a break yet. It is time I do as I've been here in the Pacific Theater for about fifteen or sixteen months already.

One young officer named Lowrie from a broken home—a mama's boy, got so freaked out by the war here that he went off his rocker in one month's time and got his lucky ass sent out of here on a hospital ship. He was a city boy-spoiled sissy. Not a tough bastard like me, the Horrible Swede. Ed "Dreamer" Fearon is now the Terrible Irishman.

Well, lets see about war news. We finally pushed the Japs out of Guadalcanal and we are moving slowly up the line. Damned slowly. Last night a lone Jap bomber dropped four bombs on an ammunition dump across the bay over at Halavo on Florida Island. They were aiming at some ships but hit the ammunition. All the base officers were called out. About twenty men were killed or wounded. I went to the radio shack then up the hill to watch the fire works. You could see flames high up in the air and lots of explosions. I saw them bring in wounded men in a Higgins boat. I went back to bed. We are in just as much danger from attack as over at Guadalcanal now.

I saw Hugh Patterson the other day. He is on the Gridley now and likes that duty. He can have his tin can duty! He is the most fantastic Scotsman I've ever seen for enjoying himself in a war.

March 3rd, 1943.

I missed many days of writing in my diary with my new duties as Head Communication Officer. I did manage to make a journey over to Purvis Bay on Florida Island. I went in a Higgins boat with Captain Kessing, our base commander. Also with us were two LCT officers. It was a wonderful trip over, the sky was clear and beautiful and the landscape was enchanting—We stopped at a native village to look over a future camp site. Saw a huge war canoe and a native Catholic church. We walked through the jungle aways then went on to a Marine camp. I made my official call then we went back to base. I then did a vigorous weight-lifting routine in the afternoon. And then came evening.

I went on duty at the radio shack and after two hours I came back towards camp. I lingered to listen to wonderful American music over the radio, looked up at the stars for a few minutes and silently said my evening prayers. And then I went to bed. My back was sore from lifting too much weight. I was in bed for about 20 or 30 minutes when BANG! BANG! BANG! Three bombs dropped out in the harbor. Baldy, Ed, and I were awake and making desperate attempts to preserve our lives by hitting the deck and getting into our fox hole. We weren't prepared for this so we nearly wrecked ourselves getting to the foxhole. I was bare naked. I got tangled up in my mosquito net and struggled for some time getting untangled, hurting my back in the process. Ed cut his face and all of us banged our knees badly. Baldy knocked my jug of papaya liquor over into the open fox hole and messed the place up in fine shape. We were a much damaged, muddy, naked and scared trio. We were mostly surprised though the terrible noise of the bombs dropping was terrifying. My heart leaped into my throat. One plane made the raid a complete surprise as it slipped past our radar. The bombs landed in the harbor near a ship and injured six native workmen. We are at the front lines alright. It looks as though the Japs are going after Tulagi now. Praise the Lord and pass the ammunition!

March 4th, 1943.

Nothing happened. Luckily we had no air raid. We got some sleep and much work done on a fox hole improvement effort. Everyone is keenly interested in fox holes and are working furiously at improving their safety.

March 5th, 1943.

The old secure feeling we had for some time is now gone. Everyone knows that we are still very much in the war. Yes, we are on the front lines. It seems to be Tulagi that the Japs are interested in bombing now and not just Guadalcanal. We got our first alarm about 9:30. I was in the radio shack. We heard planes over head, bombs dropping, and our anti-aircraft guns blazing away. We turned down the lights, secured the circuits and the switch board and when things let up a bit we headed for the fox hole. I was the last one out of the old rickety shack. The fox hole was pretty exposed as the boys hadn't figured on this. We cowered under the palm logs, and listened to the terrifying falling and exploding of bombs near by. When I thought it was over, I foolishly groped my way up to the radio shack. Some of the radio boys followed me. While we were there more bombs and guns went off. We hit the deck and more or less prayed. Baldy and Ed were on with me. They all went back to the fox hole. I went back to our tent over the hill and went to bed. I heard the next day that the PT Base was hit and some men were killed. One was a Lieutenant. Also a bomb hit at Halsey Field in a grass hut. Luckily the men were all in fox holes and saved. Another bomb went off near a fox hole and blew a man's brains out who was foolishly standing in the entrance and others were wounded. Some duds fell over by Blue Beach and luckily no one was killed there. We really laid up a barrage and claimed shooting down two Jap planes. Actually this was someone's over estimated optimism or wishful imagining. There was no proof of this.

March 6th, 1943.

The next morning there was much work being done to improve the fox holes and our new radio operating place which was in the making. The CBs are drilling us a radio room in the side of a hill so we can operate all time without turning off the circuits and heading for a fox hole. I was busy all day. I took radioman White with me going all around the island looking for sand bags, The marines had them all and wouldn't part with them. We walked around and up the ridge and found some good places for a camp away from the main base targets. I plan to move up there soon. It is no good being in our tent with no protection. Night came and sure enough CONDITION RED rang out. We headed for our fox hole—Baldy, Ed and I. We heard planes overhead and our base guns cut loose and bombs dropped but few exploded. Some dropped in the water of the bay. It is a terrible sound when bombs drop. Your heart goes into your throat and you start praying. Finally the planes went away; and finally I was able to get some sleep. This Admiral or General Patch, I think, said the Guadalcanal Battle was over in February. It was not finished here on Tulagi.

March 7th, 1943.

When I wasn't on duty, I made a trip with Baldy to my rock on the highest point on the island. I got his agreement for building a little shrapnel-proof place to get into for a full night's sleep. We could lie there with protection from hearing the noisy generators which sound like fifty planes going overhead. If the Japs came over we could just stay where we were and take no chances high on a rock. Only a chance hit could get us which would have to be a direct hit. From this rock we could look out onto the most beautiful scenery of the whole area at sunset time. It was a very inspiring location.

We had several CONDITION REDS in the evening so we tumbled into our fox holes. It clouded up later; it rained a little so we were able to sleep peacefully. Our radio tunnel has been started by the 26th CBs.

March 8th, 1943.

We had a daytime alarm but evidently the Japs were immediately taken care of—shot down or chased away. I never worry much about daytime raids. Our pilots are too good for the Jap pilots and usually shoot them down.

I talked to a Ensign Hayes, a flyer, who was on Irving Johnson's last cruise. He was a swell fellow. Also I met Lt. Delaney of Com 14 who knew Mrs. Shepardson and daughter Harriet. He was going to greet them for me. Luckily tonight, though we had an alarm, there were no planes overhead. I got some sleep and got lots of V-mail from home.

March 24, 1943.

There is a big gap here in my writing as we were into our routine of decoding and encoding messages at the radio station. I think maybe by this time the CBs had finished drilling the tunnel in the side of the rock hill for our operation. Once we got in there with our equipment we could stay on the air during CONDITION RED Jap air raids.

My Hornet survivor radio men were great as they were taking their exams and getting promoted. I would sign the papers and then they would be sent down to the Exec's office for final approval. He hadn't wised up yet as how fast I was approving of the men's passing of exams. They all deserved promotions as far as I was concerned after their ship, the great aircraft carrier Hornet, had been sunk and now with duty here with malaria and fatigue.

We had one most indispensable man. This was Lieutenant Stoddard. This great guy could repair our coding machines which were always needing repair. He was always cheerful and worked much to death. We couldn't get along without him. I wonder where he is today? Did he ever get some good duty? I wish I had kept track of him and others. Ensign Hill who had gone to Dartmouth University was a good guy too. He worked down below some place. He had family connections with their congressman or a senator so he got shipped out early. I don't think my great friend Bill Rom from Minnesota had arrived yet.

Now to get on with the events of this day. The "beach comber" lay in his bunk (a cot) behind his mosquito net. Regretfully he opened his eyes then closed them immediately. If there was anything he hated it was the necessity of painfully crawling out of the sack, dressing, and commencing his distasteful routine of being a communication officer. It was still early; the dawn with all the freshness of a tropical dawn was unspoiled by the beauty of sunrise. What a shame not to be up to enjoy the glory of the sunrise as it can only be in the South Seas. Yet the unpleasant thought of his duties caused him (me) to stretch, close his eyes and relax into dormancy. Breakfast was entirely out of question. There was strain at the breakfast table as the deadline for getting to breakfast was 7:15—much too early for an avowed beachcomber. Besides most of the food served at breakfast was repulsive. There was no escaping dreams as he did of lovelier lands and adorable feminine companions. He must get up before his superiors began to despair in finding their communicator. It was a joke to this communicator for he wished only to commune with nature and least of all with the countless details of a war which was so repulsive to him.

He shortly climbed up the hill where he could get some pleasure in watching the many lizards scamper out from underfoot. He watched the clouds explode in puffy masses over the long ridge of mountains across the bay; and a dozen other fascinations of restless nature.

With the routine of the day pushed aside, the beach comber and the Dreamer eagerly headed for the beach with two marines, Sheffield and Foote. Clothes were quickly cast aside and the four of us waded through the dirty water near the beach. Then we swam a 100 yards over waters inhabited by sharks, barracuda, and numerous other real and imaginary monsters of the coral reefs. We skirted the island and pulled ourselves up on a ledge of a small high rock island. Here with diving face plates we explored a dark underwater cave. We dove from a 30 foot cliff and then explored the fairyland on the ocean floor.

On the return trip Sheffield and I climbed a trail over the larger island over to a 30 foot ledge and down a vine to the waters edge.

Back in camp Dreamer Fearon and I gorged ourselves with chicken and ice cream at the CB's mess we luckily got ourselves invited too. The CBs knew how to get delicacies from ships as they had much "know-how" for getting things done the Navy didn't know about. What a pleasure it was to be on good terms with CB's. After watching Nugu, the pup, with the terrible bow legs walk ten steps, lie down, walk ten more steps, lie down for 15 minutes, we slowly made our way back to our tent. Nugu was named after an island way out in the main channel where we had a lookout station with several of our radio men. A dog the boys out there had puppies, one of which was this comical mongrel pup. I made several trips out there in a Higgins boat to bring the isolated boys supplies and to see how they were faring on their lonesome small island. They would give warning about any suspicious ships that came by.

With my helmet and books in hand I went to the radio shack It was a moonlight night with few clouds. After a few minutes there was the CONDITION RED signal. All hands poured out of the flimsy shack to the cave. Plane motors were heard—the damned Japs again! Our guns roared; the walls of the cave shook with vibrations and concussions This went on for some time, but the thick rock above and around us kept up our spirits most wonderfully. The routine raid was over and no harm done this night. After my watch I drifted back to my bunk in the army tent with Dreamer Fearon and great friend Baldy.

March 24th, 1943.   (Actually my writing of yesterday should have been dated the 23rd)

I got some good tan today. Wilson, a friendly officer of the CB outfit, was from Texas, like most of his outfit. Many were engineers and construction men and roustabouts for oil drilling. They could do everything far better than the Navy's way of doing things such as unloading ships etc. Well, Wilson, Dreamer Fearon, the Marine Foote and I had a wonderful swim off the rock on the tiny island. This ideal recreation suits my philosophy of life wonderfully. I traded the base Chaplin two books for one of his. I came out the best with a most interesting book named *The Dark River* by Nordoff and Hall. This book was tragic and true to life about a young Englishman who fell in love with a young Tahitian girl. The lad's uncle was a race-prejudiced old Englishman. Well the romantic book made me want to live in Tahiti and fall in love with a beautiful island girl there. Little did I realize how many times I would be going there and my friend Dreamer Fearon actually living there, building two lovely hotels.

Dreamer and I got the Captain O.O. Kessing's permission to take a Navy Flight physical exam. We were figuring out ways to get out of Tulagi. Getting flight training back in the States was one possible escape route. Actually it was Ed's idea for he was really fed up with being here in "Hell's Kitchen" as we called it. I then spent much time in the shack reading Conrad's book Lord Jim. It was a good story while I waited for the usual night air raid. This night the Japs didn't bother us

April 1st, 1943.   My Sister Patty's Birthday

I slept in the tent near the cave. I can really sleep now with a more secure feeling. Let the Japs come down now. I'm working on a Jap bayonet I'm going to send to Dorothy, my girl friend back in my home town. It's pretty rusty but I'm cleaning it nicely. Also I'm working on making a native walking stick of native mahogany. Then I was visited by the native scout back from Guadalcanal where he goes out on patrols in the jungle to kill Japs. He said he hadn't killed any on this trip.

My friend Bill Coltas dropped by. He had been spying on the Japs up at Munda and had extremely exciting adventure stories to tell. He is an old time explorer and really knows how to survive in these jungles. Once he was bombed by our planes when he had lit a fire to cook coffee! What a courageous man he is. He had collected birds on Pacific Islands for the American Museum of Natural History in New York. We celebrated a bit before darkness set in, drinking the rot gut brew we got from our messenger, Hatfield of West Virginia. (We also brewed our own rot gut stuff from fruit.) Ensign Hill had taught us some of the verses of the naughty song the Gatherin' o' the Clan which we sang. Maybe it was Robert Burns who composed this delightful song.

April 2nd, 1943.

I hung out around the safely of the radio shack near the new cave that was being blasted. Today I tried to get a poor radioman Maithew sent out, he was so wasted with malaria. I got no cooperation from our sad sack Executive officer. This guy, a fat slob of a character, seemed to care less about our poor enlisted men who had already been stationed here for seven months.

Wilson, Haun, Dreamer Fearon and I swam off our rock again. It was most refreshing and has become one of the more pleasant things of life out here—one of the few pleasures that we have. We then got some ice from Wilson, our CB officer friend, and O'Boyle of the CB's got some rum and soon I felt better than I'd felt for many months. It really paid for Dreamer and I to have some CB friends for they know how to get hold of things the Navy doesn't know how to get. We then ate a wonderful chow with the CB's. After supper we played football with a roll of toilet paper in the company streets. A big party took place in our tent where we sang again the Robert Burns naughty song of the Clan, and shot the breeze.

April 3rd, 1943.

Luckily we were able to sleep peacefully—there was no disturbing generator noise, Jap planes overhead, and condition red alarms. We rustled up a breakfast of a cup of coffee, a coconut, and some Spam. Also we bummed some chow up at radio city. I visited with my radio gang men and boys while I was at it. Then SHUDDERS! Just before noon we got a CONDITION RED. The boys headed for the new radio cave. A Solomon Island native joined in. These natives really have the eagerness for getting into the cave. They don't like the Jap bombs at all.

My skin seems to be rotting away from the damp heat. We call it jungle rot. My heat rash really bothers me but then I'm in far better health than most of the fellows. Dreamer and I listened to the Hit Parade. What wonderful music. But it does get one homesick for the many girls of our dream world and dancing with them on a cool and beautiful dance floor. Yes, then loving them one at a time. Here I was 10,000 miles away from the American lovelies. I'd settle also for Australian women. I dreamed on and prayed to get to where some of those lovely creatures lived. Then I thought of Dorothy, my girlfriend back home. I'd never dated her. I only knew her as a high school girl at a campfire girls camp when I was a counselor. I figured she had great possibilities. But it was now only imagination and hope.

April 4th, 1943.   CONDITION RED! CONDITION RED!

I was up in time for breakfast at 6:30. It is the first time I've done it for a long time as I'm a true man of the tropics, lazy. I had to put in some time censuring mail. Then I put in some time at the radio shack doing nothing. The cave isn't quite ready for us to move all our radio equipment into it. Then we got a daylight CONDITION RED. But no enemy planes. A lot of the natives crowded into the cave. They get the word quickly. They hate bombs. Ya, so do I. Then at four in the morning we got another CONDITION RED. I woke up in a hurry and woke up Baldy. Ed had the watch. I grabbed my clothes and made it to the cave in nothing flat. Everything comes automatically when we hear that awful wailing sound that Jap planes are due to arrive.

Today I worked some more on my Jap bayonet for Dorothy. I'm really getting it in good shape. I guess I really love that girl, at least in my imagination. I wonder how she will like me when I see her? I hope she does. Ed and I put up our army tent again. We had orders now to move up to the old bombed residence on the hill above us. We had two new communicators, Day and Golden. I'm next on the list to get out of here with Ed and Baldy.

12

The War Heats up at Tulagi

April 5th, 1943   HURRAH! MOVING UP TO THE RESIDENCY

It really poured down early in the morning—rivers poured through the tent. I had a very rough time. My bunk was on a slant so I kept sliding down to the foot of the bed. I got up to change location and waded through mud to do so. A big pile of dirt or sand was in the middle of the tent—it so happened that the CBs had dumped it there so we could use it as a deck. I had to dig in with my hands to level off a place. No Japs bothered us though.

Later in the morning we got a CONDITION RED so the radio gang boys moved into the cave. Many "Cave Happy" natives were in there with us too.

I went to a big ship n the afternoon and there got to drink cokes and iced coffee. I visited with Meyer of my midshipman Northwestern class. As I had only one sock to my name, I got the supply officer, a full commander to sell me six pair. He was one swell man.

We now had orders for me, Dreamer Fearon, Morris Baldwin, Greenough, Lowery, and Hill to occupy the old British Residency up on the hill. It was the best break we have had yet as it was wonderfully cool, pleasant building. I'd just as soon put in another four months here if I could live there. I will really enjoy it as long as we are permitted to stay there.

In the evening while I was in the radio shack, we got a CONDITION RED. We all rushed to the safety of the cave. After that we had a naughty song fest which lasted a half hour after it was CONDITION GREEN.

April 6th, 1943   ENJOYING THE RESIDENCE

We had a CONDITION RED about six in the morning! I had a good fox hole so I breathed freely. Nothing happened. Dreamer and I are really taking life easy here in this spacious residence. We are resting as much as possible and enjoying our big comfortable house. We read books, write letters, and eat anything good we can find. We have three new communication officers now and all are good men.

The War Heats up at Tulagi

I celebrated April 6th today with Wild Bill Rom, and Dreamer Fearon. It was an anniversary of America declaring war on Germany in 1917 and I was born on April l0th. I cut loose in the residency. Soon Wild Bill and I were dancing the schottisch and running the low hurdles. I then went roaring down to chow where luckily no senior officers were around so we were able to continue our celebration. I thoroughly amused all hands.

I had just turned in for the night when we heard the clanging bells of CONDITION RED. I dashed for the foxhole. We already heard planes overhead. our guns poured it to them. Over at Guadalcanal they shot two Jap planes down in flames, Planes were all over the area. Luckily no bombs mere dropped here at Tulagi. It was plenty thrilling but I don't advocate it for a steady diet. It was a big and busy night at the radio shack. Our Black Cats really took after Washing Machine Charlie. At the radio shack we'd rigged up a long dead yellow snake so when someone opened the door they would get a big surprise as it was attached to the inside of the door. It could very well have been a poisonous snake too.

Some of the Naval Base Tulagi, Solomons Radio Gang—young Reserve Officers in mid 1943. Lower row is Bavis, Tom Larson, and Kellogg. All at the Tulagi British Colonial Residence. Standing are left to right Bill Rom, Kid Conner, Leach in the middle, and two unknowns next to Leach. Kid Conner and Bavis were from Philadelphia, and Bill Rom from Ely, Minnesota, and Tom Larson from Aitkin, Minnesota.

Pete Fugina, Bill Rom, and Steve Habian at the residence on Tulagi in 1943.

Naval Reserve Junior officers at Tulagi in 1943.

By war's end in 1945 Bill Rom is a Lt-Comdr.

April 7th, 1943   JAP PLANES ON THE RAMPAGE AT TULAGI

Well old man! I'm not quite 26 years old. Give me three more days if I be granted that many more. Some big shot down in Noumez, probably General Patch, should have been here today if he thought the war was over at Guadalcanal and Tulagi. We'd been notified that we were no longer in a combat area. Oh yeah! That so-and-so would have changed his mind on this day so close to my birthday on April 10th.

Hot rumors filled the camp in the morning, and from our radio messages from the electric coding machines. Everyone went around with his helmet and was spotting all the fox holes along the way. I was cautious enough myself as I always think of future grand children I might sire through my kids. (Here it is July 3rd, 1998 and still no grand children from my three kids.) Well to get on with April 7th:

As we knew the El Japoes would be down today, I hung around the radio shack and attended to business off-and-on. Here I could be very near to the cave the CBs were still digging out in the side of the hill for our future radio room. I was listening to the radio with seaman Marrithew when we heard a couple of dynamite blasts. It sort of lifted us to our feet and once on our feet we drifted over toward the cave. Our telephone operator told us the condition was BIG Red! So! I gave the word and we all shoved off for the cave. Just then the Jap dive bombers cut low over the hill just above us and really went into action on a few little ships out yonder. Well, our guns and their bombs began to blast. The cave is full of men surging in and out. We cheer wildly when we see a Jap plane crash or go away in flames. The least little movement towards the deeper recesses of the cave sends us all into it with a wild rush. Americans are so curious that they hate to miss the show going on outside. That's probably why so many Americans got their heads violently detached from their bodies. Well! The cave walls rumbled and shook and planes were flying all over the island. I saw a little ship smoke for awhile. Then, the next time I looked, I didn't see it anymore. I saw a wild American Gruman pilot chase a Jap right down the middle of the harbor. He was blazing away at the Jap and our guns were blazing away at both of them. I heard later our pilot was picked up afterwards. He claimed he'd shot down seven Jap planes.

The El Japos sank the tanker Kanawa and the tin can Arron Ward. The surviving officers came up to the residence to live with us. All were pretty fair fellows. They'd lost everything they had on those ships. It was pretty exciting here today I must say. The Japs lost 39 planes out of 98 and sank three of our ships. So the score was a little better for them today. Everyone here of our radio gang is very enthusiastic about the cave the 26th CB's are blasting out for us.

April 13th 1943   A GREAT DAY OF EXPLORATION

Luckily and surprisingly I got permission to go with General Fuller and his staff on an inspection of outlaying Army posts. General Fuller had gone to Dartmouth University and was not a stuck-up Westpointer. Lt. Crookin, of his staff, had invited me to accompany them and I jumped at this wonderful chance to break away from Tulagi for a day.

We had a Higgins boat, supplies, and a small party made up of General Fuller's Com Gen of the island group. He is in command of the Fijian Defense Battalion. His staff officers with us were Lt. Jamison, Captain Walters, Lt. Crookin, and a native guide and two seamen to run the boat. General Fuller is a real man—tall, strong, and friendly.

The boat went out through the PT passage at the end of Tulagi toward Florida Island and then up the coast of the larger island. Of course I went hog wild looking at the tempting thick wild jungle that we passed. As we sat under the hot sun we trolled for fish. The native guide made a lure out of some palm stalk. He cut down the stalk and pealed it off like a layer of birch bark. This made a white lure which had a hook and it would twirl in the water.

Below Olevuga Island we turned in a channel toward an Army OP (Outpost). The General had a good strike and pulled in a big barracuda. This fish had big sharp teeth. They are dangerous and will attack someone in the water if they see something glittery on the person. Near shore we came up on a reef that dropped off into 60 to 70 feet of water. The sea life below us was enchanting. We could see large schools of fish, giant clams, sea lilies, and many colored corals. A rubber boat with two Army boys came out to us to pick up supplies. Then we went on up the coast.

We cruised past Olevuga Island and went past a number of small palm covered islands with the whitest beaches I'd ever seen. The next big island was Vitilau. This was way up in the northwest end of the island. We were closer to Santa Isabel Island, a Jap held island, then either Savo or Guadalcanal. We carefully cruised down a narrow channel. I saw a launch owned by a native chief. We stopped at Sambini Island, a small one with a native village, and an Army outpost on it. The natives here were refugees from Santa Isabel. Their village is the cleanest I have ever seen as far as native villages go. Here the Army boys were living the life of Riley.

I had a swim in crystal clear water. The General swam with us. Then while I was swimming, I saw 26 planes flying over in formation. The planes flew low over the water. Other planes circled in smaller numbers. I thought the planes were ours returning from a bombing mission up at Bougainville. I was later to learn otherwise for they were all Jap planes. We didn't know it at the time, so we swam peacefully on. The General and I paddled over to another island in one of the native alligator canoes. There we visited a church and talked with the villagers, who for the most part, were pretty naked.

I hadn't seen a fully dressed woman for a half a year now. Some of the gals were pretty well endowed, and all were more or less pregnant and with little babies suckling them for all they were worth. I got some Venus cowry shells from a native in exchange for some soap and razor blades. Then I saw something funny. An old man was paddling a canoe and behind him was a little two-year-old with his little paddle who was giving a helping hand. In these primitive villages the young learn to be useful at an early age. Then I saw several little brown babies romping in the sand. The natives sure love their children and believe in large families. We tried fishing with dynamite and hand grenades and got a few fish which floated up.

April 27th, 1943   A LETTER THE SAME DAY TO MY PARENTS

Wrote a letter the other day but it got lost for the time being so will have to start in again. Just got letters from Barb, Pat, and Virginia plus some from some women. Pat and Barb sure wrote cute letters. They sent pictures too. I wish everyone could send treats! I'm eating nuts, candy, etc. sent to my friends here from their folks and relatives. Ed's mother sends him stuff like that all the time and I feel guilty eating his when I never have any to offer him. I once got some cookies from Jim Orr's wife. It looks funny—four sisters, a mother, and several girl friends. Its hard for us to get stuff like that out here. I did get a bottle of beer from the Navy, but had the fever so I didn't enjoy it.

ADVANCED NAVAL BASE FOLD

April 15, 1943

BASE ORDER NO. 15a-43.

Subject: Daily Routine.

   1.   Effective this date, the following daily routine will prevail for all Naval Units attached to this Base:

```
0400 - - - - - - - - Call Ship's Cook of the watch
0430 - - - - - - - - Light galley fires unless
                       Condition Red or Yellow.
0545 - - - - - - - - Reveille
0630-0715- - - - - - Breakfast
0730 - - - - - - - - Turn to
0800 - - - - - - - - Colors
1130 - - - - - - - - Knock off
1145-1245- - - - - - Dinner
1300 - - - - - - - - Turn to
1630 - - - - - - - - Knock off
1700-1800- - - - - - Supper
Sunset - - - - - - - Colors
2100- - - - - - - - -Taps
```

   2.   Sunday working routine may be modified as found necessary by Unit commanders.

   3.   Colors will be kept flying at all times. At morning colors, haul the colors down just in time to hoist them at 0800. At evening colors, hoist the colors immediately after they have been lowered in colors. Whenever available, a bugler will stand by for colors.

   4.   Meals will be served promptly within the hours specified. No late meals will be served except to authorized persons or by arrangement with the Commissary Officer.

   5.   If Condition "Red" or "Yellow" prevails, this daily routine may be modified as necessary and indicated times set back by the duration of the Condition set.

                                          O. O. KESSING

Distribution:
List I.

ADVANCED NAVAL BASE FOLD

103 ~~108~~
~~102~~

April 15, 1943

BASE NOTICE NO. 29-43.

Subject: Commendation.

    1.   The following commendation from the Commanding General Fold Area is quoted for information and congratulation:

> "HEADQUARTERS
> FOLD AREA.
>
> 13 April, 1943.
>
> <u>MEMORANDUM TO:</u> All Combat Units.
>
>   1.   The concentrated air attack by the Nips on April 7, 1943, was long expected and our preparations to handle the situation have proven successful. The attack was repulsed in spirit and action worthy of the cause for which we are fighting. I say to every man who took part in the action "Well Done".
>
>   /S/ G. M. STURGIS
>   G. M. STURGIS,
>   Col., USMC.,
>   Commanding."

O. O. KESSING

Distribution:
List I.

I am just existing and that is all. My mind is a million miles away from my work and this area. I will be no good again until the day I set foot in America, Australia, or New Zealand. This tropical heat and being so confined makes a fellow totally indifferent to the life and the world. Two bottles of issued beer cheered me up wonderfully today. If we had it every day it sure would help our morale.

Ten of my poor sick radiomen got out and I'm very thankful that they did. They were survivors from the aircraft carrier Hornet that got sunk at the Battle of Santa Cruz. You have never seen such happy boys. Hope they get the STATES. If I don't soon God only knows what I'll do.

I saw Hugh Patterson for a few minutes the other day and he looks fine. He is on a ship that moves about so he gets some variety. I may see him again here. We exchange all the news. He visited with my good friends the Hagens down in Noumea and had a swell visit. They are the finest people in that little country of New Caledonia. I expect to see them sometime maybe next month or so as I'm next on the list to leave here. I never told you but I passed a physical exam for the Navy Air Corps and have put in my request for training. Should get it within six months. It is my last hope for getting back to the States and getting out of this job of communications I never have liked. This would get me about a year's time in the States. I would have to live a lifetime in that year and I would because I know how things are out here and would appreciate every moment. If fight I must, I might as well really fight. The Air Corps is made up of young progressive officers and men and not the old time regulation "waste and paper Navy". So Dreamer Fearon and I have hopes. We both put in for the training and if we could go to the same school we would be very happy.

There is hope, of course, It may come at the darkest moment. But its awful tiresome waiting for that time.

It is too bad you can't go to California and see the spring flowers around Bakersfield and up into the valleys. But you have done a swell job so far so I mustn't expect too much. You would love Zion and Brice Canyons in Utah and those peaceful little villages there. The young Mormon girls are beautiful and ride horses. Salt Lake City is an interesting place. On the way home you just watch the road carefully and think of how I stood for long hours trying to get rides hitchhiking and how I slept out in the sagebrush with the coyotes. I think of it so much and wish so much that I was there now where I belong. I can just imagine how the sagebrush smells and the views of the purple mountains. I think of the vast expanse of the clean plateaus. I'm dreaming here now as I sit in the Com shack and type from the Com typewriters all in big-letters. I walk around quite slap happy and "rock happy". I walk around in a daze from the heat and long duty hours, and lack of sleep from all the CONDITION REDS. I will close for awhile as the damned war must go on forever it seems. I have so many great and worthwhile memories.

It's the next morning now. I had a great rest even though huge rats as big as puppy dogs were making a great racket and boring holes through the big papayas we'd set out on a table here to ripen better. I also see huge fruit bats flying around at night. The natives eat them.

I feel pretty good physically except for numerous skin itches. Am getting depigmenting too as my back is quite full of white blotches as it is almost impossible to dry them out and we all have the same problems. It is lucky the way I've kept clear of malaria. I must have very good resistance against it. I do take the atabrine pills which turns the skin yellow. I expect to move out within a month now. I don't know. I will be either have good luck or bad luck. I will let the GOOD LORD decide my fate out here. Love, Tom

13

Sea Shells And Letters Home

Dear Sister Annie, May 9th, 1943

You were awful nice to send me that last letter of yours and the luscious picture along the Potomac River in Washington D.C.. When I'm living in Tahiti some day with my sweetheart, (whoever that may be), I will want you to come and visit me for a long time. Annie you would look stunning in a grass skirt with a flower lei around your neck, and flowers in your hair. I still haven't found the fellow I would want for you. He must be very choice as I love you very much Annie. Please get a tall strong fellow, a real man who has the love of the outdoors and who will treat you swell. Of course you must love him and treat him like you should. If I ever get back I will want a girl who really will love me and not give me any cold shoulder stuff. Life is too short for that.

Please write often to me Annie as I love you and your letters. When I come home some day; and if I get flight training, then maybe I can introduce you to some of my friends. I've never known Dick Lavine but he sure sounds good to me. Don't let any wise guy in Washington try to get funny with you. I really should be there to take care of you Annie. I don't trust those stinking draft dodgers in Washington.

Things aren't so bad here now. I really don't mind it much. My real complaint is that the poor Navy guys never get any leave while the spoiled Army guys in the States get all the breaks, the USO dances, the girls, and all the fun. I want some fun sometime too.

Today I went on a little tramp all by myself. I had a bottle with me with some formaldehyde in it and a can. I went down by the beach and collected some hermit crabs. I was going to hunt for little animals in the coral but the water was all dirty because of a heavy sea and wind. So then I looked for bugs; then did find some big sea shells which I can use for making bracelets like the kind I sent you and the kids from New Caledonia.

We get good food and once in awhile a bottle of Australian beer to drink. Living conditions are getting better every day. But Annie, I have been away from the States for 19 months now and it would do me so much good to get back for awhile.

It is sure swell about our victory in North Africa. Our Aitkin National Guard boys of Company B were there. Wished the war was over as wars are so stupid. Men are stupid idiots to deliberately destroy themselves in war and all their valuable resources. That's why I have little interest in wars. Did GOD have these insane wars just to cut down on over-population?

I am still collecting souvenirs and funny things as I always do. I can save a lot of money here now. I have over $550 in the bank in Honolulu. That money I'm saving for travel in the South Seas and its not to be used for anything else. You know Annie, I plan a five year trip around the world after the war. I want to get lots of good experience. Some day we can go on a canoe trip Annie-get your boy friend and I'll get my girl and we will start off. [Gad! what a sad sack dreamer I was.] Love-Tom.

May 13th, 1943.   A New Head Comm Officer takes over.

I have a good tan and feel pretty good. We had a CONDITION RED in the moonlight tonight. I was in the cave with the boys playing poker in the dense smoke. The rot gut brew jug was in the cave too that our beloved Marine orderly messenger Hatfield makes. He's an expert being of the famous feuding Hatfield clan of West Virginia. The boys hardly paid any attention to the Jap planes overhead and the mad firing of our many anti-aircraft guns., Two months ago the boys would have been scared to death. I was notified today that I am no longer Assistant Communication officer. Some new young Reserve from Harvard outranks me by a few weeks. That pleases me plenty as I have less responsibility and can crap out more and pursue my real interests of collecting seashells and souvenirs.

Well this Com officer was horrified to see the rotgut brew we were guzzling. We figured in a few weeks he would be depraved enough to be drinking it himself.

May 18th, 1943.   BILL LOWREY GOES OFF HIS ROCKER

Lets see what has occurred the last few days. Moonlight every night and that means Washing Machine Charlie will be down in the evening air. Plenty of Jap planes came down last night. They dropped bombs all around us and evidently they missed their targets by a long way. They dropped at least twelve bombs. I almost went to sleep in our radio room cave with the boys on duty. About fifty natives tried to come in with us. I think the Black Cats shot down some of the Jap planes.

I was really sharp on watch. Dreamer Fearon was sampling his wonderful bottle of bourbon and in so doing passed out the samples to Rom, Kid Conner and me. We got exceedingly gay and in a festive mood. Yes, we were the happiest we had been for many a day. We were running around, naked of course, in the residence. Wish we had more such samples.

Bill Lowery went crazy and got himself sent home. He figured a long time ago that the only way to get out of the war and the Navy was to go crazy so he went crazy. Yes, he concentrated on that and he really did go nuts. He was also sick with malaria, terribly homesick, nervous, and afraid—poor kid—I was glad to see him get out. Actually he was from a broken home, a city boy, a sissy, and not a tough "HORRIBLE SWEDE" like me.

The Future Lt. Commander William Rom with local native scout and also Navy officer Kid Conner from Philadelphia at Tulagi in 1943.

Then our humorous friend Ted Highberger got out too. He was a good kid but the Captain Kessing, the Base Commander, had a grudge against him and recommended that he lose his commission as an Annapolis officer. We were all envious of him. He had an extremely "dirty" mind, and entertained us constantly with his funny jokes and songs. If he had been a reserve officer like the rest of us I'm sure the Captain wouldn't have cared what he did. But evidently Annapolis officers were supposed to be far superior to us lowly reserves. Ya, join the Merchant Marine and get a white man's square deal. Some fellows got all the breaks.

I was really out of my head today with no ambition and terribly in need of a woman, some love, and some real living, most of all I want to be a free and self respecting man and not a miserable serf to the damned military feudal system. I long for the day when I'm free.

Well yes! Of course I had fear of being bombed and killed. We all did. We would drink about any kind of alcohol, beer, whisky if we could get it, torpedo alcohol, and rot gut brew. I had a secret place up on a hill where I would go where I thought I'd be safe from Jap daytime bombing. I carried a little New Testament on my left shirt pocket. And I wore a small totem pole cross on a braided necklace for good luck and to remind me of my North Woods worship of nature. Oh yes, I prayed plenty to survive the war. If I was fatally wounded I wanted to die in my Minnesota buckskin jacket. I was no "Gung Ho" Annapolis officer war monger as they had been taught to be. I was just a lowly reserve.

June 4th, 1943   From Devil's Island Tulagi

Dear Mother and Dad, I addressed a letter which was really my diary. It went as follows: "On watch now and not too busy and not too miserable for writing a letter. Am just getting over a head cold I got from the cooler spell and the abundant humidity here. So am almost back to normal. Life goes monotonously on day after day and year after year. I spend much time these days reading many books I may not ordinarily have read. That is one advantage I do have which lots of time to read—so I read. At present I am reading a book called: *This Above All*. I had seen the show out here five months ago. The story of it is very real to me and the sentiments the same. Joan Fontain played the woman's part. When I get home I will hopefully find a few Joan Fontaines and really be in Heaven while I can.

This war has given me a very different outlook on life. I now believe in living while one can. Ya, Heaven on Earth. Right now I'm living a most non-existent life. If I ever get back to civilization there will be no time to waste aimlessly. I will try to live life to the fullest.

Dreamer Fearon and I got a dispatch off to Washington requesting flight training and orders. We figure that that is our best chance of getting out of this HELL HOLE, some States life again, and getting into something worth while. I think I have a fair chance of getting flight training orders within the next two months. It would let me be in Heaven for a year of flight training at any rate. It's my only hope. However, if I don't get flight order training I won't be too disgusted anyway. Right now it is hope. Life without orders would still go on. I wouldn't be too disgusted. Its a dog's life out here now the way we are treated here. Being kicked around doesn't phase me. I just don't give a dam for nothing bothers me outwardly, but inwardly I despise and curse the whole military system. Luckily I manage to keep out of trouble pretty well as I'm on to the foul Navy Annapolis regular officers and all the regulation bullshit. But, of course, I pray for the day that I'm out of here. I tell you though, I'll never be the same again. I have very definite opinions and plans for the future. It will take some time to get adjusted again back in the States and civilization.

Say Pappy—I've never heard about sister Jinny's new addition to the world. If I hear nothing about it I take that it is a girl. Otherwise I'd expect some word on it rather soon after it all happened. (Later I learned it was a boy, Stuart Patterson. It was named after Dr. Stuart Patterson, the Navy doctor father from Brainerd, Minnesota.)

June Fourth continued....

I will have to knock off smoking some day. I have nervous work so I smoke a pipe, plus cigars, cigarettes and anything I get hold of. I smoke but only spasmodically though. It wouldn't be hard for me to give it up for a nice woman when I get home. Many of the boys here are feeling bad. Some have been here for ages and are getting out of their heads. They have high hopes of getting out of here but were now just told by the high ups that they have to stay here. No relief in sight for them yet. It is awful hard on these young radiomen boys I tell you, and especially when it is not necessary for them to stay here forever.

I just received a letter from the Wolfs in San Pedro—my great friends. They wish they could have seen you while you were in Arizona. I got your Grand Canyon letter. You have my permission to ride a mile down the canyon on a mule. That would be pretty good for a fellow like you who has been sick so long with your bad arthritis. Now I don't think I'm much interested in a National Grand Canyon Park job because it is a government job. I really want to be on my own, ya, like a trip around the world after the war. I tried for two years to get a job there and got no response. So I say TO HELL WITH THEM! However it sure would be a good job

I guess you must think I'm pretty outspoken and wild? Yes, one gets that way out here. I guess no one could stand to have me around very long. When I get out in the woods for awhile back home, I'll cool down a bit. Sure! I'm lonesome for the piano when mother plays and some of my favorite songs. I would love to dance to some real smooth music too with a queen of some kind or other. I have plenty of spirit left for when I get home. I will be pretty bewildered when I hit the docks in San Francisco in "48", as the song goes. But I will recover almost immediately.

I got a religious book from Aunt Lillie and Ethel but will get much more out of the book I'm reading now—*This Above All.* I don't care to read these religious books as I can do much better sitting on my rock up in the jungle clearing getting inspiration. My religion is in all of beautiful NATURE anyway. The Christian's world seems to be always fighting and is very greedy.

My good friend Morris Baldwin got his regular weekly box of candy from his beautiful wife. Wish I had a wife or somebody to send me some. Hope to have better luck in the next war. Love-Tom

June 16th and 17th. THE BEACHCOMBER FROM DEVIL'S ISLE

Dear Grandkids,

I was enjoying a hot sun bath in the old Tulagi winter time. I lay out on the grass sweating and looking up at the blue sky and white puffy clouds, looking at the pretty flowers, the ships in the harbor and the blue water and the green jungles. It was all very peaceful and beautiful. Then we got CONDITION RED. 120 Jap planes are headed down so we get all set to see a big battle. We didn't wait for long for soon we saw many enemy planes over toward Guadalcanal going after some of our ships. The coast watchers always give us advanced notice of enemy planes heading our way. The Japs were dropping bombs all over—and our ships, guns and the many shore batteries were really going after them. Our planes really gave them hell and shot down 77 Japs to our losing only six. It is hard to believe it when you hear it but I was convinced it was true. Yes! I saw it all happening. Saw lots of blazing Jap planes diving into the water.

That evening I saw the show with Dorothy Lamour. It sure great to see that beautiful woman—to see what a real sexy woman looks like even if it was Dorothy Lamour. Then sure enough, we got another CONDITION RED so I grabbed my helmet and hit out for a fox hole. The Jap planes came low in the moonlight and our guns gave them everything they had. I've never heard so much shooting for a long time. We claimed we shot down at least two for sure. How so? The Japs should know by now that it isn't safe down here. Their bombs all landed in the water. I then hit the sack for an hour then went on the mid watch.

June. 17th, 1943.

It was a beautiful day. It was too good to be going to a communication class dreamed up by the god dammed Annapolis officers. I should have been off swimming for good health. It was funny when I first came up here I was fighting in a WAR. Now it is going to classes. We reserves really resent the Annapolis regulations they dream up. They think we must read up the boring Navy regulations. They know nothing about psychology and recuperation for guys in this malaria-ridden Hell hole. Us reserves really despise Annapolis officers who think we are lower class Navy citizens. That is why we call USNR the "you shall never returns".

It was censor mail for awhile then we chowed down. Then Dreamer and I went to the same show again. The moon was so bright it seemed to burn up the sky and the palm trees all around us. Just being beautiful was not enough word for it. It was hauntingly so as we looked far out over the sea to Savo Island where the ghosts of thousands of dead men were deep down in that infamous sea. It was a HAUNTED SEA.

Back at the residency Dick Hill played the organ in the blackout room. I danced an Indian war dance until the sweat poured off of me. Stoddard jitterbugged, and we all sang and hollered and drank some of Tom Stoddard's beer. We really managed to have an enjoyable time. And this night the Yellow Bastards let us sleep.

June 30th, 1943   EXPRESSING MY WAR OPINIONS TO SISTER BARBS

Got your letter of June 10th Annie; and sure liked it very much. It is sure nice of you to write to your old brother who is all mossy and decayed from jungle rot. Dreamer Fearon says that's nothin compared to the Solomon Island sores that he has. At last I'm officially an uncle now that Jinny finally kicked through with a boy baby. He has a hell of a name-ya, Stuart Patterson after his father, the son of a hell fire and damnation Presbyterian minister. I'll give him a good nick name. I told Jinny that I didn't like the names of any of her kids. Let's see. What will I name my kids? They will be Jack, and Dick, and Bill, and Ben, and Pete, and Tom and then for the girls—Sylvia, and Diana, and Sonia, and of course—Barbara Annie. They will be scattered around of course, but all healthy and cute fellows.

Here are more of my sentiments. Gee! You are havin' a good time. You lucky girl. I wish they would let the women fight the war and let the fellows stay home on account of then there probably wouldn't be any war. Oh well! Kill um' all and be done with it-ya, all the healthy men and common people. Let all the rich, and cripples and diseased and perverts live to carry on the human race. This will give you some idea what I think of war.

I've never been to Coney Island like you. Gee it would be fun. I could really go wild there. I do like New York for having fun in it but never to live there all the time.

Now some day Annie, I want a beautiful mountain valley where my kids can run wild all over the country side on their ponies—pintos—and grow up natural and beautiful. And I'll do everything I can to keep them out of any cursed future war.

Stuart Alexander Patterson! What an awful name for a cute little kid that doesn't mean any harm to anybody. Lets see, what would I name him. Jinny nick names him sailor. Huckleberry would be a swell name for the little dear. Do you remember all the Indian names I gave you once? Well, I don't. Its swell though that it is a boy cause it proves that one person in our family infested with girls can still get a boy. Jinny wants us all to get busy so we can all have our kids together. But, I say nuts to that. The rest of us—Marj, you, Pat and me can wait awhile and we will all then have our kids at the same time.

I plan to be married a few years before I have any kids. I want to show my future wife the world first. I'm pretty lonesome for about any girl now, but my best girl must love the woods, the outdoors, travel and a vigorous adventurous life. Otherwise she would never be happy with your brother out here in the Solomons. Well Annie, I want your advice on the girl for me and I give you advice on a boy friend for you. We can do this as we are such good pals. Mother and Marj would pick the wrong kind for me. They have too high falutin ideas and Dad might pick too much of a goody goody type. You and Pat might like the kind of girl I'd like.

Now Annie, listen to old brother. To hell with those sailors and guys running around Washington. Have your fun yes! But somehow I think that forest rangers out in Wyoming are your type of man. I always trust and like a fellow who lives in the woods. Please give me Dick's address. I can write to him at his home address. Of course you know yourself how you feel. But somehow I think Dick Levine is a swell fellow. Please be good to him Annie. I'd even approve if you were out in Wyoming with him now in the west instead of Washington D.C. He'd love you and take good care of you and you would live in God's country.

Some day when I can find out for sure who my girl is I'd marry her and really try to give her a happy life, and of course she would have to be the type that likes me. Well Annie, its really up to you. Marry who you rightly love and tell the family they can go to hell if they don't like it. If the family doesn't like my girl, I'll clear out and of course also tell them to go to hell too. I don't care what most of the family thinks. You are the only one whose opinion really matters to me. Then I know Dad would like whoever I liked as he is that way.

We have shows again—and its all wonderful for us here. I see every one of them many times as they show it. I saw *Holiday Inn* twice and loved it. The beautiful girl and the music *Road to Singapore* was great too with Bob Hope. It was a real vagabond movie. See Annie, I'd sure would like you and Dick to visit me in Tahiti some day. Wouldn't it be fun?

Thanks for writing Annie. I'll write to Dick now. Lets get a new name Stuart Alexander—yes, something more human. Love to you Annie and to Pat too.

14

More Letters Home and Souvenirs

August 20th, 1943   GETTING OVER TO GUADALCANAL

Dear little kid sisters, Guess I will start a little letter to you and am in hopes that I get to finish it tonight. I use the radio cave typewriter which prints in block letters the way we record our messages. I may get to finish this letter if we don't have any routine disturbances such Jap air raid. I'm down here with the boys tonight.

I've had plenty of adventure lately. Had some very interesting and much very tiresome and unpopular duty for me. I have some Jap souvenirs. A Jap skull I found myself, a Jap helmet, part of a parachute, and some small stuff. It happened this way. I had a few days off to see things twenty miles across the Iron Bottom Sound to Guadalcanal. I went across in a small motor launch. I stayed with some Army outfit and heard some of their stories. I went to a Palm Sunday service under the trees. You should have seen the trees. They were all full of lead. I wonder how they got there? Sure by guns.

An Army officer drove me way up by the Matanikau River where many Japs had been slaughtered. I had to look out for booby traps. I found dead Japs. The ants had eaten out the brains and soft parts leaving the skull clean. I scraped off the hair of several and dumped them into a gunny sack plus a nice helmet I have to this day. A guy is pretty far gone when he begins to collect enemy skulls. The Army officers wanted native souvenirs so I promised to get them some. Think of it! Getting liberty over in Guadalcanal.

I saw some of the spookiest sights one could imagine. They were far worse than the things you read about in newspapers back home. I wish I could have taken some pictures.

August, 1943.   ANOTHER LETTER TO SISTER BARBARA-MY FAVORITE

Dearest Annie the Barbarian,

Another night. I have the midwatch, Annie, from 12 to 4 in the early morning. Guess what? I skinned a seven foot snake today and rigged it up to the door of the radio shack to give entering people a bit of a scare. The snake was a beauty and could have been poisonous too. I'm going to tan it as it will make a good souvenir.

Here I'm known as the local beetle and butterfly, snake, seashell, and lizard authority. My reputation as such has spread around through the South Pacific. Even brought a sack full of Jap skulls back from Guadalcanal. I gave some to friends, and kept one for putting my helmet on and my pipe in the mouth. The Protestant Chaplin tried to get me to give the poor thing a Christian burial. I told him he was Shinto and I needed his skull where I put it. The Catholic Chaplin didn't try to get me to give it a Christian burial. I suppose he thought I was pretty far gone—ya, rock happy, the way I was staggering around.

Before I got orders to leave Tulagi and take flights down to New Caledonia and thence to Auckland, New Zealand to become the Liaison Officer of HMNZS Leander, I will write about a few events and adventures I had not recorded in my off-and-on diary writing.

I must tell about the PT Boats we would see coming out of their base up along Hutchinson Creek. The brave crews would leave in the late afternoon so by evening they would be out in Sea Lark Channel and the Slot to fight any Jap ships. Ensign John F. Kennedy was among the PT boat commanders. Of course his story of PT Boat 109 is well known how he rescued his men. Then, of course, he became President. Some of the young commanders of the PT boats were Ivy league boys who had had experience with sailboats etc. Others like a good friend of mine from the University of California had to learn from scratch. This was Bill Mills. I'll tell about him soon.

Well Dreamer Fearon, Bill Rom, and others of my buddies would get a boat and cruise up Hutchinson Creek to the PT Base where I had friends. There at their officer's club we would drink Torpedo juice cocktails. This would be a tough drink with lemon juice and some of the torpedo fluid alcohol in it. This was deadly stuff and more than one man out at Tulagi died of it by drinking too much. We knew when to stop drinking that famous or infamous stuff. The Navy wouldn't issue us regular liquor like the British Navy gave their tot of rum to their men every day when possible. We in America had too many religious and puritanical parents who would raise hell with the Navy and Government if they let us have liquor to ease our pain and fear. That's why we would drink any kind of dangerous rot gut brew we could get our hands on.

Now about this Bill Mills, a so-called friend of mine. He became a great war hero. Bill had been in several classes with me back in Berkeley at University of California that spring semester of 1941. He had taken a course about the Inca of Peru with me taught by a very infamous professor Ronald Olsen, a real drunkard fun guy.

Bill came from a military family and had a younger brother who was to major in Anthropology. Bill joined the Navy and took training to be a PT boat skipper. He was a Gung Ho fighter with lots of fighting guts even though he was short and sturdy. He even wrote to one of my sisters when I'd write to him about the war I was in and he was still not yet in the Navy.

Bill hated the Japs so much that once he was in command of a PT boat he would really go after them. He invented the idea of attaching a mortar on his PT boat then going up close to shore at night at Jap held positions and lob shells into their camps. One time he rescued a Jap from the water and this treacherous character pulled a gun (pistol) and tried to shoot Bill. Well, Bill had to shoot him and dump him in the water to the sharks. After that Bill would never pick up any more Japs in the water. He sank many of their troop barges and accounted for many of their men.

Later when I heard his story when he visited me at Naval Air Station Livermore in 1944, 1 heard his tale of great heroism. He was operating up along Bougainville. He was hung up on a coral reef but managed to get his boat off it. Then another PT Boat got stuck on a reef so he attached a cable to it and started to try to pull it off. The wind was about to drive his boat back on the reef so he grabs an axe to cut the cable. The cable snapped back and got stuck in one of his legs. He is about to bleed to death. However he was gotten to the medics. His leg had to be amputated and replaced by a wooden detachable leg. He was given awards for great heroism.

I don't remember if he was allowed to get back on a PT boat or not. At any rate we kept up our friendship after the war. He graduated from Cal then went to Stanford Medical School over in San Francisco.

I even remember visiting him over there when I was going back to Cal in 1946–1947. We were still friends mind you. When I came back from my African adventures in 1951 or 1952, Bill got the idea of going back to Africa on an expedition with me. I had no money for this but got the impression that he would finance it somehow and I would lead him. He was about to intern up in Michigan someplace. I was to visit his World War One veteran father in Arizona who had a hobby of collecting interesting semi jewel rocks. I stayed overnight at his father's place.

I'm sure his father advised him very strongly and wisely not to go on any Africa trip with me as I had depended on Bill to find ways to finance the trip. He'd even given me some money to come to join him up in Michigan—U. of Michigan, I think. I got half way there then no more money from Bill. I never heard from him ever again. His dad had told him for sure not to be a fool and try to go to Africa with me. Years later I read in Time magazine that a Dr. Bill Mills up in Alaska had been fishing in a small river and his wooden leg came off and floated away. I don't know if he still lives. Anyway he turned out not to be my friend. At least he could have told me why he had chosen not to try to go to Africa with me. I took a very dim view of this kind of a friendship as we had been close friends.

On the 16th of October 1943 1 was promoted to Lt. J.G. by ALNAV. I didn't buy my new officer bars as I thought Jap snipers loved especially to take pot shots at American officers. Also I'd gone around the bend so far that I'd wear hibiscus flowers over my ears and go to the radio station and around the base shirtless. Eventually we got more and more regulations by the Annapolis officer.

TALL TALES FROM THE SOLOMON ISLANDS

On November 30th, 1942, 1 had arrived at Guadalcanal from New Caledonia. As I had a day at this famous island before going over to Tulagi, I interviewed some sailors, pilots, and Marines to take down some of their stories of the war. I begin as follows;

The contributions are from sailors who have fought in the numerous sea battles around here, and Marines, and soldiers up on the front lines of Guadalcanal and Tulagi. These stories are of daring rescues and escapes, of desperate and bloodthirsty fighting, stories of the natives and their part in the war and of their life. The fantastic scuttlebutt is prevalent for Sailors and Marines. Most of the stories are true accounts from eye witnesses; others are the fantastic imagination of shell-shocked boys gone half crazy. Some of these wild stories have been passed on to many people so that they have reached gigantic proportions. Many of these give the humorous side of life in the Solomons, and others the terrible tragedy of it all. Though some of these stories are not accurate, I write them down here as I heard them from men who claimed they were true.

1. My first story was related to me by Lt. Farnam from Minneapolis, Minnesota. Back in October and November of 1942 Farnam was transferred with his P-39 Fighter Squadron from the airfield at Tontouta of New Caledonia to Henderson Field at Guadalcanal. Those were the days when the fighting was the toughest on this island of Death. Every day at regular intervals the Japs would send over planes above Guadalcanal by the score—sometimes as many as 40 planes in each wave. Of course few of them escaped our deadly fighter planes and our anti-aircraft batteries.

One day Farnam and his squadron was sent out to strafe enemy positions on Guadalcanal. He was flying low over the tree tops and giving the Japs all the hot lead he had from his guns. Flying thus he picked up a few machine gun bullets in his engine from the Japs on the ground. Suddenly his motor went dead but he continued to head out over the sea. About two miles out from shore, his plane crashed into the water. Luckily he escaped from the wreckage and swam to shore regardless of sharks and Japs. He landed on a wild beach within Jap territory. He was dead tired by this time so staggered up on the beach and hid in the jungle. He walked for many miles in the jungle until his shoes wore out and soon his feet became so sore he could hardly walk. Luckily he didn't run into any Japs. In the course of his feeble and painful struggle to push on back to the American lines, he came to a river. Here he found a native canoe. In his attempt to steal the canoe, he was discovered by some natives. These friendly natives with their tippy and slender canoe succeeded in paddling Farnam back to the American lines by traveling by sea at night. Farnam got back to the American lines after a week in which he would never forget and at a time when he expected at any moment would be his last. When I saw Farnam back at Tontouta, he was none the worse for his wild adventure and was very happy to be alive.

2. Of course there is the story of the Marine who came upon a Jap asleep under a tree. The Marine did not shoot the unfortunate Jap nor did he take him prisoner. He kicked him soundly until he was awake then ran his bayonet through his belly. To kill a Jap in his sleep would be too kind to a treacherous yellow belly bastard according to that Marine.

3. There was also a marine who was in the habit of collecting the ears of dead Japs. He was unmolested in this practice until his collection grew quite large and began to stink. Finally his commanding officer had to put a stop to this rather unique hobby.

FIRST ENDORSEMENT   U.S. NAVAL OPERATING BASE, NAVY 132.
P16-4/00   6 November 1943.
From: The Commanding Officer.
To : Lieutenant Thomas J. Larson, D-V(G), USNR.
Subject: Change of duty.

   1. You reported this date.

   2. You will further proceed and report to the Commanding Officer, HMNZS LEANDER, for duty as Communications Liaison Officer HMNZS LEANDER.

                              G. T. Rains

Left Guadalcanal 0700   1 November 1943
Arrived Noumea N.C. 1500   1 November 1943

   Travel performed via Government Plane.
   Government quarters furnished in Noumea.

Left Noumea, N.C. 0700   4 November 1943.
Arrived Waipapakauri N.Z.
                  1800   4 November 1943.
   No Government quarters – plane forced down
                bad weather.

Left Waipapakauri N.Z. 1000 5 November 1943.
Arrived Auckland N.Z. 1130   5 November 1943.

Disbursing Office
U.S. Naval Supply Depot
Auckland, New Zealand

ADVANCED $60 on 18/11/43
which should immediately be checked by the disbursing
officer taking up his pay account, and the checkage
reported to the General Accounting Office and to
this office.

PV-226-44 LT. (jg) G. A. Smith, (SC), USNR
DISBURSING OFFICER.

Thomas J. LARSON.

SECOND ENDORSEMENT.

Reported H.M.N.Z.S. "LEANDER" 6th
November, 1943.

                            Immanuell Lt Cdr RN
                                  ACTING CAPTAIN.

Relieved of duty H.M.N.Z.S. LEANDER
5th JANUARY, 1943.

                            Immanuell
                              ACTING CAPTAIN

15

Out of Hells Kitchen at Last!!!!!

When I write the war book from records I've put together there will be some things which I will remember which didn't get recorded. Dreamer Fearon had preceded me out of Tulagi. Down in Noumea he'd gone to ComSoPac and told those people of personnel I'd been there far too long and needed to get out. Thank you my good friend. Ed then was sent home on a Navy ship. Soon after he got home he married the beautiful Mary Rae MacArthur.

When I went over to Guadalcanal to catch a plane for Noumea, I wouldn't go to the Communication Quonset hut to see Gaylord who had sent me up here in the first place. He got his punishment by being sent to Guadalcanal.

I stayed overnight at Guadalcanal, then the next day was on a transport plane- DC-3 or DC-4, and was winging down to Espiritu Santo (Button), and thence to New Caledonia to Tontouta Airfield just 30 miles north of Noumea. I was riding on the back end of a truck. The only other passenger was the most gorgeous Army nurse I'd ever seen. As I hadn't seen or talked to a nice nubile white woman for so long I was dumbfounded and speechless. But I still remember that kind Angel of Mercy for our wounded men. If I had gotten my wits in time I could have talked to her, then dated her, then married her and eventually the two of us would have been forever happy and still in love. But, the shock of seeing such a BEAUTY was more than I could handle. Ces't la vie!

Back in my beloved Noumea at last, I was put up in Navy transit quarters. I hadn't kept a diary and I don't remember the details of where I stayed in Noumea. I do remember I saw my friend Lt. Bud Ranier who most likely was the one who got my orders for me. I was cursing ComSoPac quite loudly and he had to calm me down. At any rate Bud was still my good friend. Years later in about 1993 or 1994 or even later we got in touch. He and his lovely wife visited us; and we visited them in Seattle when our son Tom lived at Des Moines near Seattle.

I went immediately to see my good friends, the wonderful Hagen family. They had been so kind to me and even let me store all my souvenirs—a huge box of them with uniforms, seashells, Jap things. I had rifles and a forty-five, a 38 pistol, and some books and sundry other things. These I got shipped off to USA and eventually the shipment caught up to me when I had duty at Naval Air Station Livermore, California. It was fond farewells. I was never to see Albie Hagan nor his gracious wife ever again because I didn't get back to New Caledonia until 1992. Also I said good by to Poulette Baumier, my lady friend. She too had died of cancer before I returned to New Caledonia. I found her beautiful sister Andrea in 1992 and got information on Poulette who had a child from an American G.I., then married a governor of Wallis Island and had lovely children. Also I found Peter Hagen in 1992 and his gracious wife. Upon my arrival in 1992 at Tontouta Airport, they got me to the Youth Hostel, gave me much hospitality, and two times I went up north with them to their farm.

In early December I was winging my way with my duffle bag southward toward New Zealand. This was an epic journey I'd always remember—There were a few enlisted Navy men in the plane with me. The DC-3 or DC-4 landed at Norfolk Island far out at sea east of Australia. What a beautiful country club island it was. It was a two hundred foot mesa sticking up out of the Pacific Ocean. Here grew the Norfolk Pines. I lay under them to look up to see little birds running along the limbs of the majestic trees. Golf courses were all around, and club houses, and a few villages. Our pilot was having the plane refueled so we wouldn't be here long. I wanted to stay in this beautiful paradise forever.

I learned later that the Mutiny of the Bounty people descendants came here for awhile, then packed up and returned to Pitcarin's Island. It was reluctantly get back on the plane and it ran right off a cliff at the end of the runway and was off over the ocean. And then I soon was in the stormiest journey on a small plane I'd ever experienced and survived. We were bounced all over the sky and ocean like corks on a rough sea. It was one harrowing journey. I may have had something to drink to lessen the anxiety I had about landing in the sea. It was one scary trip. Fortunately the young pilot was good and finally we were over North Island of New Zealand, that promised land. The airfield was at a place called Wapepikouri or something like that. We were to fly on the next day to Auckland where I was to report to the HMNZS Leander for duty as the American Liaison communication officer. I was taken to a hotel in a village here near the airport. I was told there were Yugoslav immigrants living here. A Maori girl, a maid, wanted to be very patriotic for the cause of the war and to help me, an American ally, by giving me her generous body in sexual bliss. I was all in favor of her idea but then an old man who evidently was in love with her told me she had venereal disease. Too bad! It wasn't true of course. And I missed having a wild and wonderful evening. Then the next day the airmen on the plane told me about all the fun they had at a dance and making love with 14-year-old girls.

A short flight over beautiful green New Zealand soon had the plane at the Auckland Airport. I got my duffel bag and a suitcase with a minimum of clothing and souvenirs and reported to the ship. I was taken aboard and introduced to Lt. Clark the American Liaison officer who I was to relieve. I remember he was a redhead of medium built; and had been well liked by the British aboard and New Zealanders. He had been indoctrinated properly and had been assigned to the duty perhaps from New Zealand. I, on the other hand, coming out of the wartorn Solomons after eleven months of suffering all the heat and war conditions was not given any indoctrination instructions as to the customs and expected behavior on Her Majesty's ship. I was soon to be getting myself in trouble.

Leftenant Kier the communication officer, a New Zealander, took me in tow. I had met his brother on the Kiwi up in Tulagi. Kier was of about thirty years of age, middle sized. and very businesslike and not unfriendly to begin with. I met the only other American called Sparkey from New Jersey who was a radioman. We hit it off immediately. I was given a room and introduced to a Marine of the British Royal Marines. This elderly gentleman had been in World War One with all kinds of medals. He would bring me hot water for my morning face wash; bring my tot of daily rum; shine my shoes, and all kinds of embarrassing tasks which I felt I should do for him instead.

The ship would be in port for eleven glorious days. The crew and officers were ashore during the day and many lived here and had wives and families living here. Only a skeleton crew would stay on the damaged ship. She had been torpedoed in the bow by a Jap long lance torpedo in the Battle of Kolombangaro up in the Solomons. I would learn later of the ship's history before coming to the South Pacific.

Back up in Tulagi harbor I had visited John Fernading who had gone to my Northwestern Midshipman School with me. He was an officer on a transport ship. He and others told me about all the wonderfully beautiful and eager young women waiting for me in New Zealand. I'd written their names and addresses into an address book. I now looked forward to finding some eager girl friends in Auckland.

At this time I had only a very minimum of duty in the Comm center aboard ship. I could go ashore on liberty and report back to the ship before midnight. That same day I'd reported aboard, I was up the street to the Thistle Hotel. I had my address book with me. I met the Proprietor of the little Hotel who was an Irishman. He announced to me that for Yanks all drinks were on the house. But being a strict Catholic none of his many children were permitted to drink. He was a most kind man and appreciated that the Americans had come to New Zealand to protect their country from the Japs.

With strong liquor in hand, I sat down in a small pub-like room. Here were a number of most attractive young ladies all of whom could easily drink any liquor deprived young American G.I.'s under the table in no time. It was now I met the adorable and wonderful young Doris Mears, of Irish decent. We hit it off right away. Furthermore she had a car. I would get liquor from the ship's canteen and she could get "petrol" for her car or was it vice versa. I forget which it was. Any way we could operate together for dates. The next day at noon I would meet her at the Thistle Hotel and she would take me for a drive out into the country of gorgeous New Zealand. Also at the Hotel I learned a great Irish toast for drinking. "Most astonishing good fortune!" I liked that one.

As Doris drove far out into the beautiful green hills covered with flowers and lovely trees, I was in glorious Heaven in my anticipation. I'd heard from many G.I.s from ships up in Tulagi Harbor how eager the New Zealand girls were for love as all their best men had gone off to war and many of them killed. The girls were desperate for love from the many love-starved Marines and Sailors from America. We had a nice bottle of whisky and Doris had put up a little lunch for us.

We stopped the car along the road next to a beautiful meadow full of flowers of many colors. Little traffic came by as petrol was rationed so we would have privacy. Hand in hand we went out in a field and sat down to lunch and happy nips on the bottle. Soon we were kissing passionately. Off came our clothes which laid on the grass. I caressed her lovely ample sweet body as she pulled me down upon her. Long we loved with flowers above us. I was in Heaven. God had finally rewarded me in full in the form of an Angel from Auckland.

Back in Auckland, we went to Doris's home where she lived alone as I remember. By the fire in her fireplace we lay on the floor and loved again. All the window shades had to be closed. Doris told me that an older man had an obsession about her and was stalking her. I must be careful as he was very jealous about her though she despised him. She drove me back to the ship and I was aboard before the stroke of midnight.

In the morning the Royal Marine—a most distinguished gentleman—had poured hot water for me, shined my shoes, and greeted me cheerfully. How undemocratic was this custom of the snobbish British Navy. I went to breakfast in the wardroom and met some of the junior officers. No one had warned me about not talking about women in the wardroom. That was about all I could think of for talking about; it about the main topic of interest in the wardrooms for junior American officers. I stupidly did mention the names of some of the young ladies I had addresses for in my little address book. Some of these women could well have been wives and sweethearts of some of the New Zealand officers. Finally someone gave me the word. Also I'd circulated with the enlisted men of the ship especially some of the Petty officers who invited me to have a meal with them. This was unheard of for British officers. The biggest mistake I made was that I had a Jap skull from the battle field of Guadalcanal in my duffel bag. I was told to get rid of it. Yes, get it off the ship! With the lame excuse by them that the Maoris on board were superstitious. The bow had been hit and some men aboard had been killed. That afternoon I presented my skull with the sea shell cat's eyes opercula's of the Turban shell to a curator at the Auckland Museum of Natural History.

Then Doris and I visited a hotel where we got a room so we could become more intimately acquainted. I heard much laughter in the hallways as girls and Marines went from their rooms pursuing each other. The hotel was a beehive of young lovers running from one room to another. Soon many of these fine young men would die at the invasion of Tarawa. They would leave many of their children in New Zealand. This was the last fun fling for many of them.

Doris and I had more trips out into the country, visits to the Thistle Hotel, and loving by the fireplace at her home. On board the ship I met a kindly British officer who was the Executive Officer. The crew called him Bulkhead because he was not very bright. We became friendly and I gave him some of my precious seashells. The Captain was nick named Black Mamba because he could strike like that deadly snake in all directions. I would encounter him later.

In 1996 I had an article published in the Guadalcanal Echoes which mentioned that the Captain of the Leander was another Captain Bleigh like the one on the Bounty. The article had been read by an ex member of that ship by the name of Harry K. Hutton of New Zealand. In it he said the Commander I referred to was Stephen Wentworth Roskill of the Royal Navy. He became Captain of the Leander after the return from the Battle in the Solomons at Kula Gulf. Our Captain Manserge who was promoted to Commodore and returned to Britain, thus S.W. Roskill became Captain. He was an expert in damage control and it is through him and our boys that the ship was saved and returned to New Zealand. Nobody crossed swords with him and survived the ordeal as many of our boys would know. The late Captain Roskill was a Naval Historian, Gunnery officer and navigator.

I was to have my encounter with Black Mamba later when Leftenant A. had stabbed me in the back and was sent up to face Black Mamba when I was innocent of losing a page out of a British secret code book.

The happy afternoons and evenings soon came to an end with the kind and generous Doris Mears. I sent a letter up to my good friend Ensign Kid Connor still in Tulagi that when he got down to Auckland, he must look up Doris which he did and she also favored him with her generous and patriotic love. GOD BLESS DORIS FOREVER.

About mid November of 1943 Leander left Auckland and was headed up toward the Panama Canal in the vast Pacific. I remember some islands soon after we left Auckland with many sea birds on it. My duties as Liaison officer was in the communication code room with my radioman who was called Sparks. He was a nice young man and we got along fine. Also the New Zealand radiomen were nice fellows. That treacherous communications officer was a hustling busy-body. Another New Zealand officer who had to perform duty at encoding and decoding messages was a thin scrawny supply officer, a real snippy pipsqueak who would soon show his nasty treacherous colors.

All was well for awhile as we headed slowly up toward the Panama Canal. The ship was to be delivered at Boston Naval Yard for repairs to her bow which had been severely damaged by the Jap torpedo. I got along fine with the middle-aged British Marine who waited on me in my room.

Before we got to Bora Bora Island enroute, I heard through the Communication office news that our Marines who had been resting up in New Zealand, had landed at the island of Tarawa where there had been a terrible battle and many marines killed. I'd probably met some of these Marines in Auckland where they had been busy leaving their offspring behind to become New Zealanders. How sad. Michener in his book: RETURN TO PARADISE had a chapter about New Zealand in it and the predicament of the New Zealand women with all their best men gone off to war.

Sometimes I would sleep on deck under a gun turret but the fumes from the stack gave out poison. I tried exercising with an officer who conducted this morning activity. I was still groggy from my ordeal of living at Tulagi and should have avoided this activity.

I now quote from my booklet: *BORA BORA HISTORY AND G.I.S IN PARADISE* as follows:

The New Zealand light cruiser HMNZS Leander on a late afternoon of early December in 1943 limped through Teavanui Pass of the barrier coral reef of Bora Bora island. During the naval battle of Kolombangara in the middle Solomon islands on the dreadful night of July 13th, 1943, she had been hit by a Japanese torpedo on her bow. Now she was on her way to the shipyard in Boston, Massachusetts, for repairs. On the passage from Auckland, New Zealand, I'd been assigned temporary duty as the American Liaison Communication Officer.

Coming up on deck I was immediately spellbound by the magnificent view which struck my eyes. High above me rising in sheer cliffs and clothed in a verdant green mantel were the monolithic truncated twin peaks of Mt. Paaa and Mt. 0 Temanu. Surrounding the majestic mountain was a coral reef with a guardian fringe of low palm-studded Motu islands which protected the emerald island from the great sea around her. Only through the one narrow opening in the reef could ships enter and depart.

Was I dreaming? Never in my life had I seen such awe inspiring beauty. Coming from the war-shattered island of Tulagi for me it was like entering heaven from the inferno of a living hell.

As the crippled ship glided before the mountain massif, with the setting sun flooding golden light upon the waters of the lagoon, I thanked my Guardian Spirit and the Tahitian High God Ta' aroa for a safe passage to this sanctuary for ships and men. Here was the hurriedly constructed staging base for our convoys on their way to Australia, New Caledonia, and the terrible Solomons far to the west, that graveyard for so many of our ships and men.

It was not until the next day that I was permitted to go ashore for a few short hours. Walking along a coastal road under feathery palm trees, I came upon an American Naval Officers' Club. It was the working time of day so I only had the bartender to keep me company. As I sipped a cool beer I looked up over the bar to a giant mural of the twin mountain peaks of the island. I became enthralled by the spell of the glorious painting and vowed that one day I would return to this most beautiful of all South Sea islands.

The next afternoon the crippled ship slipped out through the reef. My heart remained behind in Bora Bora as her twin peaks of an ancient volcano slowly faded away from view. As the ship cruised out to the north, with Tupai atoll to the west, I took my last look at the heavenly paradise now far away in the distance. The sun sank swiftly below the western horizon, and once again the damaged cruiser was alone in the vast Pacific Ocean.

Out of Hells Kitchen at Last!!!!!

Sparks the American radioman who served on the HMNZS Leander enroute to Boston Naval Yard for ship's repairs. He had two days ashore at Bora Bora Island enroute in December of 1943

Since that day it had always been in my mind to return to Bora Bora. But fate was to intervene for many years, for unlike some of the fortunate American G.I.'s stationed on the island, I did not have a beautiful Polynesian vahine to return to.

It would not be until 1976 that at last I was able to return with my wife Carolyn to Bora Bora. It was at that time as a social anthropologist that. I became interested in what happened to the children of the-wartime Polynesian mothers and their American G.I. fathers. After 1976 I was able to make nine more visits to the Society Islands to interview the now far scattered children who now in 1998 are in their fifties.

The damaged cruiser was alone heading for the Panama Canal and then in the dangerous Atlantic where German submarines were lurking. While the crew and petty officers treated me in a friendly manner, some of the officers were getting snobbish. I got along fine with "Bulkhead", the not very bright Executive officer who I'd given sea shell gifts. As we neared the Panama Canal the treacherous Communication officer Kier had it called to his attention that a page was missing from the cumbersome British code book. Not yet had I been accused of losing it which, of course, I had not been responsible for losing it. But someone had to be blamed.

As it was known that I had studied biology in university, someone in authority on the ship got the stupid idea that I should give a running commentary as we passed through the jungle-swamp parts of Panama. I was expected to describe over the ship's loudspeaker about the animal and bird life we were seeing. How stupid this was. I didn't know the correct names of any of the birds; and we were not on a pleasure cruise. In 1940 I'd been here in Panama on my glorious midshipman cruise. Then I could have had no idea that I would be on a British cruiser.

We got out into the Atlantic where we had luckily an escort of two U.S. destroyers. Also now Leftenant Kier was going crazy because of the missing page in the code book. Someone had to be blamed so me being the only American officer on board, I was to be the scapegoat. Kier got very nasty. I should have defied him but by this time my long ordeal at Tulagi had worn me out pretty much. Kier got the word up to Captain "Bleigh, Black Mamba" and I had to go up to face this tyrant. He gave me a sound bawling out. I should have stuck up for myself and told him that Kier was stabbing me in the back as the only American officer on board. Up at the Captain's quarters was an American General with elephantiasis from being infected at Bora Bora. He could see how "Black Mamba Rosskill" was unfairly treating me. I was in disgrace, of course, for breaking so many rules of the ship—yes, no one had been kind enough or had the forethought of giving me an indoctrination for British officers' rules on board. Their cast system I was unfamiliar with; and that Jap skull in the duffle bag got me in trouble in a hurry. In the wardroom an officer began to tease me as a Yank. He was friendly and I didn't mind. But then someone told him to lay off the Yank. I could hardly wait to get to Boston and to get my ass back in the American Navy.

We were coming from summer in New Zealand into winter in Boston. It was very cold on board the ship and the poor seamen had little comfort in this caste-ridden British ship. The comm. Officer and the snooty little supply officer were being most obnoxious to me. As soon as we got into Boston Navy yard I had the job of taking the American communication publications for burning as the ship was to go into dry dock for repairs. I met a nice young Navy Wave officer who assisted me in the burning of the secret documents. This nice young lady, an Easterner, invited me to a Navy daytime reception party at a big Boston hotel. How nice of her. Now I was eager to get off the miserable ship as soon as possible.

Out of Hells Kitchen at Last!!!!!

I presented myself at the office of COM ONE. I spoke to a young man junior officer and told him I was coming from the Solomon Islands and wanted to get back into the American Navy as soon as possible. He told me, "You must talk to Ensign Gilbert who wants to meet a man from the faraway Pacific theatre." I replied: "O.K. my pleasure." Then lo and behold Ensign Gilbert, turned out to be a gorgeous and beautiful Wave Ensign. I am dumbfounded. She told me she was so happy to meet a man who had fought in the South Pacific for at her headquarters at COM ONE none of the young men had seen any action. Then she told me: "You are invited to a party tonight and with me." I saluted her smartly and replied! "Yes Sir Mam!"

By this time I finally got my papers from the ship's clerk—the nasty whippersnapper of that supply officer who had stood some of the communication watches. He was nasty to the end. I should have slugged him in the guts. I just wanted to get off that poor miserable ship as soon as possible. I then took quarters at a seaman's' hotel for officers. I had quarters now until I could get—await orders for an assignment on an American ship or duty station. I was ready now for the Angel from Heaven, beautiful Powers Model Ensign Agnes Gilbert. She took me to a party. She was unbelievably wonderful. She was from someplace in Kentucky. I fell in love with her immediately and she loved me too. BUT! She unfortunately was a CATHOLIC. As much as we kissed and embraced there could be no sex unless we were married! How sad and unfortunate. Here I was on my way to marry that ICEBERG Dorothy way off in Los Angeles.

I even went to the Catholic church with Agnes and sat up in the front pew with her. She considered this a most gracious thing on my part. There were more dates. But by this time I was still weakened by my long ordeal in the Solomons. The weather was cold December now. I came down with flu and a fever and ended up at the Naval hospital. I was quite wild I remember with fever. There one nurse was so beautiful and treated me especially well when she heard I was from the faraway Solomons. I fell in love with her. I remember her as a tall dark haired young woman, so beautiful, so lovable. And me planning to marry a girl I'd never dated and knew only by her letters and when she was a grade school girl back in my home town. I was really out of my head. Oh yes, Lovely Agnes Gilbert came to the hospital to see me. How lucky could I get? Agnes was a gracious "Dream Woman" so sweet, so kind.

I got myself cured soon and left the hospital and headed down on a train to Washington D.C. to go directly to the Bureau of Naval Personnel to ask for orders. Then to visit my sisters, Barbara and Patty, who were employed there by the Federal Bureau of Investigation. I took up quarters in a guest room in a vast woman's dormitory building where my two sisters lived. From there I made my way to the Navy Personnel Headquarters. I was directed to a wonderful Regular Navy Commander who had been a survivor of the ill-fated heavy cruiser Quincy sunk on August 9th, 1942 in that great defeat by the Japanese up off Savo Island.

This kind officer told me I could have any duty I wanted as I'd put in two years of war duty in the Pacific and especially at Tulagi and Guadalcanal. I told him I wanted to go to an airbase in California where they had good food. The Commander said he knew just the place for me. It would be Navy Flight Training Base at Livermore, California. There at the BOQ was the ex Commissary officer of President Roosevelt's yacht. I replied yes, that is the duty for me-NAS Livermore. My orders were made up to report there in a month after I had leave. I just couldn't believe my great good fortune. How wonderful to be back in the American Navy.

While having a few free days in Washington, I visit my young sisters Patty and Barbara who are working for J. Edgar Hoover of the FBI. Patty lives in a dormitory with 600 young ladies. But Patty remembers that I used to love to hike out in the woods in all kinds of weather. Curse it all. All I wanted to do was stay at her dorm and bask in the beauty of all those young women. Instead I was obliged to tramp in slush and snow on that "bloody" hike.

I'm next off in a packed train heading for Atlanta, Georgia. Wounded and weary military men wouldn't give up their seats for the adorable young women in uniform. My sister Marjorie is stationed at the Naval Flight Base as a link trainer for pilot trainees. From NAS Atlanta I hitched a ride by plane to Abilene, Texas. The beautiful woman pilot has me sit with her in the co-pilot's seat. I am falling in love once again.

More surprises! At the Air Base in Abilene six fantastically adorable young women greet me enthusiastically as the welcoming committee for all returning war veterans. Remember that wartime song? "They are either too young or too old?" Well, I was so stupid that I end up without any of the lovelies. I had no idea like today how I would go about loving six women and how could I just pick out one like the one in the Thistle Hotel in Auckland?

Now I am a Comm officer once again with ten Waves under my command and glorious weekends in nearby Berkeley and San Francisco. But after a year-and-a-half I get patriotic again and volunteer to go back to the War. And I could not put up with the lawyer administrative officers from Oakland who dreaded having to go out to the War.

Soon the hapless Swede finds himself on the USS Lexington aircraft carrier getting repairs up at Bremerton across from Seattle.

Soon Swede Larson is running zigzag courses on the bridge and in charge of Repair Four of the Deck Department. We cruise up and down off the coast of Japan with the vast fleet of both American and British ships. Downed American pilots picked up by submarines in Tokyo Bay are sneaked into my room. I had the great forethought of smuggling a whole sea chest full of hard liquor into one of the storerooms I was in charge of. Needless to say I was a most popular Swede with the new squadron.

The concussion of those two glorious secret bombs are felt 200 miles out at sea. We steam into Tokyo Bay where I'm soon passing out candy bars to poor little Japanese children in bombed out Yokasuka Naval Base. A tanker comes alongside to refuel us. The Commander of a fleet of four tankers is Hedly Hanson, my old Norwegian first mate of the S.S. Pat Doheny back in 1938. Crossing on a breeches buoy I present Hedly with a bottle of whisky. He presents me with a Jap rifle.

The War is over! We won! And I now have enough points to return to the University of California to study for a degree in anthropology And yes! God Bless President Truman who gave the word to drop those two bombs. My only regret is that I didn't get to meet and shake hands with our great editor of the ECHOES, Ted Blahnik, when he had a gunny sack wrapped around him when the survivors of the Helena were brought down to Tulagi. Sorry Ted. Wish you had been with me at Abilene, Texas that night to come up with ideas how to handle those six welcoming ladies.

BRIDE WEALTH IN THE SOLOMON ISLANDS

Published in the Guadalcanal Echoes By
Thomas J. Larson

Back in the Guadalcanal and Tulagi campaign days of 1943 when there were no women side by side with us up front like now days in our military forces, there was still that urgent need for them.

For twenty big tins of corn beef and ten bags of tobacco, I could have became the proud possessor of a young Solomon Island woman. I smile at the thought today but in those long ago days I was quite interested in the idea. Oh yes, I really didn't know just how I was to take care of the young woman I had in mind even if I did have enough corn beef and tobacco for the deal. Then too, even if I could liberate enough corn beef and tobacco there wasn't anything in Naval regulations that covered such a case to my knowledge. Being very much of a free spirit I wasn't much concerned about Navy regulations anyway. Furthermore old Chief

Patrick of the village of Tambagaga over on Florida Island across from Tulagi, stated in Pidgin English that part of the agreement was that I had to marry the girl with a proper church wedding, and in his church.

It all started back in January, 1943. The Japs were very busy trying to chase us out of Guadalcanal and Tulagi. Furthermore I had little time to get away from my radio station on Hell's Kitchen, as Tulagi was called in those days, to go visiting native villages in search of dusky young women. The idea occurred to me while I lay awake during one of my sleepless nights. I was aching in every bone and muscle in my body and wringing wet with sweat from Dengue fever. In addition to that, to make matters worse, there was Washing Machine Charlie to worry about. He had a way of slipping in at night over Tulagi to drop bombs before one could scramble madly into the fox hole under the coconut logs.

A few days later I was over at Halavo Beach, the new seaplane base, to do a little lying on the fine coral sand beach and to bargain for some fresh fruit from the Florida Island natives who hung around there. I was still very weak from the after-glow of Dengue fever thus was not back on the watch list as yet. One had to be almost dead before being taken off any watch list in those days when everyone was sick with something or other. Though Dengue fever didn't often kill one outright, it always made one wish he were dead.

While I was reclining leisurely under a palm tree, I met Johnny. He was a very dark-skinned native boy who was in the laundry, fruit, and souvenir business. He must have been about five feet tall and had very kinky red hair with a hand-carved wooden comb stuck in it. Many of the Melanesian natives put lime in their frizzy hair to keep out the bugs and to give it a glowing red color which would be the envy of many a State-sides flapper in those days. These also were in the days out in the South Seas when a fellow could make a pretty good bargain with a little soap, tobacco, and tins of corn beef. Not long afterwards, when the Army finally arrived to help the marines, everything was a flat dolla or five dolla. I bought seven large pineapples, three big papayas, and a bunch of sweet thick bananas, a few Tiger cowry seashells, and was well satisfied with my loot.

After carrying on a very broken and hilarious conversation with Johnny, which consisted mostly of sign language, I remembered my ambition to give bride wealth for a native woman to see if it could be arranged, and to win a bet with the boys over at the radio shack on Tulagi. Not even the most passionate of young men like myself, who had not seen an American woman for over a year, was that eager to possess a Solomon Island woman as they usually appeared in those days. Not that they weren't beautiful in their own way, but they didn't exactly come up to our pinup girls like Rita Hayworth, Maria Montez, Maurine

O'Sullivan, and Delores Del Rio which hung on the wall by my bunk in the old bombed out British colonial residence building on the hill.

When I mentioned woman or "Mary" to Johnny, he chuckled loudly and appeared to be very interested. After exchanging several comments about the divine creatures I had in mind, I tactfully asked him if he thought the chief of his village might be interested in accepting my bride wealth for a young woman. My dark-skinned friend did not appear too certain about my idea but thought that maybe some big tins of corn beef and tobacco might do the trick. He promised me that the next time I came over to Halavo with some big tins of corn beef and bags of tobacco he would take me to his village of Tambagaga.

A few days later, when there was a short lull in the continual air and sea battles, I managed to trade a watch with one of my friends and was over on a Higgins boat to Halavo with a gunny sack full of borrowed or "liberated" tins of corn beef and some tobacco I'd bought. Halavo was several miles from Tulagi. To get there one had to pass Gavutu Island, then Tanambogo and Palm Islands, and cross over a part of Iron Bottom Bay. Somehow I could never quite associate violent death and destruction with the beautiful jungle and blue coral reefs of Florida Island. I found Johnny busy making a big deal with a Marine. When he had sold his immediate stock of sea shells, beads, and bananas, he beckoned for me to follow him down a swampy jungle path.

Being a naturalist and ardent traveler, I took a great interest in my surroundings. To a Marine or soldier at the front lines, the jungle could be a fearful and terrible place where sudden death lurked behind every leaf and tree trunk. For me the jungle was a paradise of flowers, birds, butterflies, and fascinating slimy and creeping creatures; and a welcome relief from the Navy radio station on Tulagi with its irritating, nerve-wracking machines and secret coding devices. True, there may still have been a few Jap snipers in trees in the vicinity, but they would hardly jeopardize their position to take pot shots at me, so I thought. I was too absorbed in all the wonders of nature that grew all around me to worry much.

The trail led through a labyrinth of countless species and forms of plant life. Huge grotesque looking hardwood trunks rose a hundred feet or more above us, Thick banyan trees with their numerous sucker branches which grew down to take root gave the trees the appearance of a community. Fragrant flowers grew in great profusion attracting vast numbers and species of busy insects, especially the brilliantly colored butterflies. Honey birds darted in and out of huge blossoms in a tireless search for nectar. Many varieties of parakeets and pigeons squawked and cooed in the tops of tall palm trees. Hanging vines and rank vegetation grew so thick that it was impossible to progress once off the native trails. On the ground little lizards scurried out of my way. Weird bird calls echoed hauntingly through the dark steaming forest in a manner that made one's hair stand on end. It was a favorite trick of the Japs to imitate these deep forest birds.

After a short but heated tramp over the muddy and twisting native trail, we came upon an opening in the jungle. We crossed this natural field of shoulder high sedgy grass until we came to a dense grove of mangrove swamp which bordered a narrow bay called Hutchison Creek. To get through this obstacle, I was obliged to crawl on my hands and knees and to drag the sack of corn beef and tobacco as best I could. I was rudely startled several times when large land crabs hurriedly crawled over my shoes or hands to take refuge in holes they had dug in the coral. We came upon a native dugout canoe which had been skillfully shaped of thin sheets of wood and cemented together with a waterproof native glue. The bow resembled the head of a crocodile while the stern had a long tail which was curled straight up about four feet. The inside of the tail was lined with a row of white sea shells called egg shells. Along the gunwales down to the waterline, were intricate designs all inlaid with mother-of-pearl shell. Johnny told me to sit down at the bow and handed me a narrow sharp-pointed paddle. As we slowly pushed our way through the mud of the mangrove thicket, I heard a loud splash and saw a dark body disappear under the water not more than fifty feet away. It was a large crocodile which had been sunning himself on a layer of coral which protruded above the water.

Paddling a narrow Solomon Islander canoe is not as easy as it appears to be. If you rise to your knees in a fairly comfortable position, you will be almost certain to capsize the canoe. And paddling in a sitting position is an awkward operation until one has had considerable practice. The small paddles require many more strokes to get the same results as one of our own north woods of Minnesota broad-bladed paddles.

As we headed out into a narrow bay, I noticed many strange looking structures made of long poles fastened together at the top and looking much like an Indian teepee. These Johnny told me were fish traps. The bay now narrowed as we slowly headed toward the village. We followed a beautiful coral reef along the shore as I saw myriads of little fish of every color of the rainbow. Above us the jungle rose on two sides like a solid green wall broken only by a few cleared patches where the natives had their gardens. Though the tropical sun beat down on the jungle unmercifully, so humid was the soil from daily rains that faint clouds rose from the surrounding hills like smoke.

At the far end of the bay which narrowed into the mouth of Hutchison Creek, I saw the village. I counted about 25 native huts along the swampy shore. All canoeists in the vicinity quickly discontinued their fishing and paddled toward Tambagaga village to see who Johnny was bringing with him. As we came closer I saw several of the young girls who were stripped to the waist vanish quickly into one of the houses. Solomon Island women in those days were not treated as equals by their men. Unlike Polynesian women of Tahiti they were not looked upon as man's better half. Thus marriageable young women were jealously guarded from all strangers.

By the time we had beached the canoe, the entire male population of the village had gathered. I shouldered the gunny sack full of precious corn beef and tobacco and waded ashore through the mud. Johnny led me before an old cadaverous-looking man who was Patrick the chief of the village. Most of the natives in this village had been influenced by New Zealand missionaries and had English names as well as names taken from their own language. Ancient Patrick, who wore only a rag around his middle, had a short clay pipe sticking out of a mouth full of broken red teeth, extended a bony hand to me in welcome. I noticed that all the natives except the very young had red stained teeth from chewing betel nut, a mild narcotic. Many of the people were infected with a scaly skin disease. Others were infected with horrible-looking running ulcers caused by a spirochete. With large soft brown eyes numerous little children shyly peered out from behind their elders, half in fear, half in curiosity. As a token of friendship I offered Patrick a package of tobacco, then rattled off my best Pidgin English plus a few words in their own language I'd learned from Johnny. Patrick grinned from ear to ear with pleasure upon receiving the tobacco while his fellow tribesmen broke into spasms of laughter at my attempt to speak their language. My new friends having now lost all of their suspicion of me; and the tiniest pickinny who could walk, now toddled close at my heels as Patrick proceeded to show me his beautiful little village. The Japanese had been so brutal and sadistic in their treatment of the natives here that the people were distrustful of all military men until they learned that the Americans meant them no harm.

Before making any attempt to barter for a woman, I knew it was best to gain the confidence of Patrick and his people. Thus I was willing to have them show me what they would in their village. First I was permitted to see their church. This was a long structure of carefully thatched and woven banana and palm fronds with many intricate designs. Surprisingly enough of these many-layered buildings were airy and cool inside. The interior of this primitive temple, founded by missionaries of the London Missionary Society, was beautiful in its simplicity. Hand-carved wooden benches faced the altar in two sections. A large wooden cross stood behind the altar. The cross as well as the furniture was inlaid with mother of pearl and cowry shells. The walls and isle were decorated with freshly cut flowers and palm fronds. Translated into their own language were Bibles. From the church I was taken into one of the private dwellings. An old woman with several young girls were busily grinding up nuts into a meal from which little cakes were made. I noticed a half dozen land crabs with broken legs protesting violently because they were about to be thrown into a fire to cook.

In the midst of my tour of the village, a sudden downpour of rain sent us all running for shelter. Daily cloudbursts occurred here without the least warning. While Patrick and I waited for the rain to subside in a shelter to store canoes, I noticed two powerfully built ebony black native girls dressed only in scanty grass skirts shoulder a heavy dugout canoe and walk off with it as though it had little weight at all. What I saw would have made a proud sweater girl, even Jane Russell, blush for I swear that there was not a bra on the American Market that could have adequately contained what those two powerfully built young ladies proudly possessed.

Chickens, dogs, and pigs roamed at will throughout the village. In great profusion bananas, palms, papayas, and many other fruits grew as well as the carefully cultivated gardens in the nearby hills. All the crops were grown and harvested by the women. I was now taken to the school where the naked students sat on a woven platform of reed mats while they recited their lessons. Beautifully designed mats covered the earthen floor whereas in the homes the ground was left largely uncovered. Bowls and dishes were carved of native hardwoods while drinking cups were made of coconut shells cut in half.

One generation ago these villagers had been the victims of fierce cannibals and raiding head hunters. Now they were peaceful people who had been "saved" by the ardent New Zealand missionaries. I noticed several pitiful human wrecks who had ugly open sores unattended for flies to feast upon at will. Satisfied at last that I had seen his village of Tambagaga, old Patrick sat down in a little clearing among the palms and his people gathered around him. I offered everyone a cigarette from the eldest man to the youngest pickininny present. By this time the men, and even the shy young ladies, had lost all fear and suspicion of me and came out of their houses to claim a cigarette. While photographing these enthusiasts for Lucky Strikes, I looked over the belles to see which ones might be unmarried and available. After a brief scrutiny I could readily spot the married women for they were pregnant, carried a small baby; and many had long razor-strap breasts which hung down almost to their waist.

I now diplomatically approached Chief Patrick on the subject of negotiating for the bride wealth needed for a wife. To my amazement the old gentleman showed no surprise; while many of the people gathered around us began to giggle. Patrick carefully explained that to give proper bride wealth a man must give many porpoise teeth and long strips of red beads which were their traditional money. It was difficult to get porpoise teeth and took much painstaking work to make beads from a special kind of rare red coral. I then explained to Chief Patrick that though I didn't have any porpoise teeth or red beads, I did have some corn beef and tobacco.

At that time corn beef was considered a great delicacy by the Solomon Islanders which they couldn't resist though a Marine or Navy man would become violently nauseated at the thought of having to eat any of the stuff. Never for a moment did I really think that these people would part with one of their precious women. So when old Patrick hesitated, I began to get a little worried. What if the old guy would make a trade and I would suddenly find myself with a dusky young maiden on my hands, especially like one of those I'd admired carrying the big canoe. After considerable deliberation on Patrick's part and growing uneasiness on mine, the old gentleman held up one hand and counted on the fingers of that hand four times. Yes, for twenty big tins of corn beef and ten packages of tobacco I could have a wife. I smiled with great relief for all I had with me were six tins of beef and five packages of tobacco. However all was not lost for I, with this trade stock, bought a model canoe, many sea shells, a war club, and a gunny sack full of delicious pineapples, bananas, and papayas. I bid a happy farewell to all the population healthy enough to follow me to the boat landing, and once again Johnny's crocodile canoe delivered me safely back to Hell's Kitchen Tulagi.

A Solomon Island (Melanesian) woman

For bridewealth payment a possible bride.

LT. Tom "Swede" Larson at WARS END ON Way home on Eniwetok Island-1945.

Somehow I never did get back to Tambagaga to deliver twenty tins of corn beef and ten packages of tobacco to pick up my promised bride. The war activity increased considerably the next few months. Besides suffering from fever, fatigue, and loss of sleep and weight, I had frequent nightmares. In these wild dreams I always saw fierce warriors coming after me with red teeth and skin covered with ugly ulcerous yaws wielding huge war clubs for my audacity to think that I could possess one of their young maidens. These rather startling dreams, usually a premonition of a Jap air raid, sent me rushing headlong into my foxhole under the coconut logs.

Ten months later, when the Navy was kind enough to send me home on rehabilitation leave, I was married within ten days to a beautiful girl I hardly knew and was seven years younger than I. Before arriving at Tulagi I was a sworn bachelor. By the time I was six months on Hell's Kitchen I was corresponding with at least ten adorable American girls I'd known from my recent college days. One of them I'd sent a grass skirt from over on Halavo. Much to my surprise she sent me a photograph of herself and her gorgeous body lying out in that skirt on her front lawn. I'd lined up all the photographs of the ten prospective wives and past playmates and picked out the one in the grass skirt. And I lost the bet with the guys in the radio gang at Tulagi.

May 1, 1995
Ted Blahnik
Guadalcanal Campaign Veterans
P. O. Box 181
Coloma, MI. 49038

Dear Ted,

A lot of interesting things happened on Tulagi which I'd like to Share with you and the Echoes readers. We had 18 air raids over Tulagi during April, 1943, mostly nuisance raids by Washing Machine Charlie. He kept us awake many nights, so Lt. Rosenberg (from New Orleans) cooked up an idea to set up a generator and a string of lights at a small banana plantation on Florida Island just to the north of us. Horrible Swede Larson and I went along with him a few times to refuel the generator. We didn't have a single night raid after this.

I noticed a picture of the HMNZS Leander in the last issue of the Echoes having been at Beirut in 1941. Horrible Swede Larson after 11 months on Guadal and Tulagi was the Liaison Officer on her in 1943 when she went from Guadal to Boston for repairs. The skipper made Swede throw his Jap skull overboard

(Actually I presented it to a museum in Auckland) and he requested a transfer when the ship arrived at Boston. Swede had filled in the eyes with plaster of paris and a pair of cat's eyes (the opercules of the Turbin sea shell), at the head of his bunk while on Tulagi. Each time he walked by, Chaplin Blackburn placed a helmet over the skull. Swede didn't appreciate this.

Also read in this issue about the 20,000 missing pair of shoes. I may have had a pair of these but they were too small and as a result of constantly walking downhill with them on Tulagi, I developed an infected ingrown toenail. I had this cut out later at the Navy hospital in Bremerton where the surgeon also circumcised me, presumably because he needed the practice. I was sore at both extremities.

The Army requested 20 LCT's from the Navy on Tulagi to move personnel from Halavo to Savo Island. We had only four on hand and I was in charge of the movement. We did it in one day by doubling back five times. As a result of this "bright" idea I was transferred back to Guadal as assistant operations officer and put in charge of all small patrol craft. I liked this duty as one APC was skippered by a college friend and he had a good supply of medicinal brandy in those small bottles. I visited him every time he anchored off Lunga Point. One SC pulled in from Espirito Santo, and I sent him over to Halavo for fuel and fresh water. At the torpedo net at the gate to the harbor, they sounded a Jap sub in waiting for the gate to open and dropped their depth charges, bringing up a surge of oil. Scratch one sub.

Whenever we ran out of torpedo juice from the PT Base, we had a seaman named Hatfield from West Virginia who had a still cooking back in the jungle to keep us supplied with happy juice. He had connections with the mess where he obtained prunes, sugar and other condiments for making moon. It made our stay on Tulagi a little more bearable. I was on Tulagi for seven months, Swede for eleven months. Most officers came and went in four months, supposedly the maximum stay required.

Our Executive Commander Jones was a little tyrant. I took the guard mail boat around the harbor one day and got nailed by him. He made me write out in long hand the chapter in Navy Regs on leaving the base without permission twenty-five times (a little humiliating for a full lieutenant that I was at the time).The ExO and the Port Director were buddies until the Port Director drowned off the main dock. He was a merchant mariner and he'd visit the merchant ships in the harbor. They could carry liquor. He came back one day in a boatswain mate's uniform and the boatswain had his officer's uniform on, both polluted. The next time he came back to base he and passed out on a tug tied loosely to our dock. In the morning only his hat was on the tug. His body came up three days later. At the same spot a seaman had dived down 40 feet to tie a rope on a outboard motor that had fallen overboard but he ran out of air before surfacing, and he went back down again, the end of him. Ensign Duckworth spotted the Port

Director. We had a PBY Dymbo hit a reef off Gavitu upon landing at night and sank with all 9 aboard. I was detailed to pick up one body that surfaced and took a new 38 revolver still on his belt, dutifully turning it in instead of keeping it for a souvenir. A second body washed ashore, half eaten by fish when we found him.

The tanker Kanahwa went down at the harbor entrance during one of the Jap air raids and the skipper beached her. My little station was the little cement hut the size of a thunder box at the main dock where survivors came ashore, some with burned skin-hanging down from their arms. The Kanahwa later sank in deep water. That day the Japs also sank one of our destroyers heading for Halavo and a New Zealand Corvette in the harbor. One minute she was there and the next, only her screw was visible with about 50 men swimming toward shore. I ordered a boatswain mate to take the ambulance down to meet them but he refused to leave the shelter during the heat of the air raid, a court martial case, but I couldn't blame him. This was the day about one hundred Jap planes hit the shipping in the slot and around Tulagi. The Horrible Swede got the tail wheel off a Zero that bit the dust.

How many of you remember the beautifully landscaped biffy our Skipper had on Tulagi? Rivaled Forest Lawn cemetery, with an oak seat and all. O.O. Kessing (OOK the Omnipotent) was a square guy however, compared with our Exec. The latter skippered the U.S.S. Shaw after Pearl Harbor, the first warship to be restored with much publicity. Rumor had it that he had run it onto a reef and was demoted to shore duty to Tulagi.

After seven months on Devil's Island and two on the Canal in 1943, I returned there in 1945 as First Lieutenant and cargo officer on an attack transport to pick up a load of troops and K-9 dogs. We proceeded to Ulithi where every one had a last fling with the beer you could drink in two hours, when being told our next stop was the landing on Okinawa. We were able to board the damaged carrier Franklin while at Ulithi.

On April 1, 1945, Easter Sunday, we anchored off the on Tan airport and debarked our troops and hot cargo. We had the fleet record of unloading our 26 landing craft in 13 minutes. Kamikazies were buzzing around and battlewagons were blasting the beach, including the U.S.S. Maryland, a ship I had been on for 13 months previously, the sister ship of the West Virginia, took a direct Kamikaze hit. We were there for six days. Maneuvering at night to avoid submarines. On the way home we got the word that FDR had passed away on April 12th, a sad communiqué. I was also the First Looie on the carrier U.S.S. Bismarck Sea which was sunk by the Jap Kamikazies off Iwo Jima, and losing half the officers and crew. Luckily I was transferred off her to the APA detail just before she was sunk. My last duty was at Naval Headquarters in San Diego in operations. By then I was married and had our first child, who is now 50 this year and head of the pulmonary and critical care department of Bellevue Hospital in NYC. And who was our best man? The Horrible Swede of course. He just happened to be stationed at nearby Livermore Naval Air Station when we were married at Grace Cathedral in San Francisco.

ONE more note...much was said about the three Sullivan brothers being killed during one sea action, a sad commentary. The little town of Ely, Minnesota where I lived lost 55 KIA's including 4 Mrace brothers in WW II. Kate Smith mentioned it on one of her programs. By the way, the walleyes will be snapping this way in a couple of weeks.

Sincerely,

Wild Bill Rom

Epilogue

EDWARD J. FEARON

"I am only interested in the future and not the past." This emphatic statement I'd heard many times from Ed my great friend of World War II days. I will attempt to write a rather incomplete epilogue for Ed. We, of his close friends from Tulagi days, gave Ed the nick name of Dreamer. His pale blue eyes seemed always to be dreaming of the paradise island—TAHITI—where he was destined to make his home.

Edward J. Fearon was born in 1920 in Santa Monica, California.

During the Great Depression years of the thirties Ed learned to work hard, and to assist his father in the construction business. Living close to lovely beaches and the beautiful bathing girls who inhabited the golden shores, Ed found his calling early. He became a great surfer, and was an early pioneer of surfing. As one of the few surfers of that period, his story was even published in the *New Yorker Magazine*. Also he was a life guard and saved many a young lady and others from drowning. His great love of the beach, swimming and surfing influenced him to move to Hawaii and eventually to Tahiti.

After graduation from High School in Santa Monica, Ed enrolled at nearby UCLA. One summer he and a friend hitch-hiked and rode on top of freight trains all the way to New York City. Ed was a very bright student and he got an appointment to attend the NAVAL ACADEMY AT ANNAPOLIS. The war had started and Ed thought it would be finished by the time he would graduate from "Boys' Town as he mockingly called it. He resigned from the Academy, and then returned to UCLA where he earned his Navy Ensign commission from the University's Naval Reserve Program. The Naval Academy didn't have a beach where Ed could surf.

It was about September of 1942 when a handsome, blue-eyed new ensign joined our COMSOPAC staff of communicators on the USS Argonne anchored in the vast Noumea, New Caledonia harbor. Ed was assigned to my watch in communications and we soon became good friends. We had pretty much the same happy-go-lucky philosophy of life. We would go on liberty together and explore fascinating Noumea the old French penal colony and capital of New

Caledonia. At every opportunity we made trips out into the beautiful countryside where we would swim in the lovely deep rivers and ride Australian cavalry horses. Those adventures will appear in a book I intend to publish some day entitled NEW CALEDONIA AND LIFOU ISLANDS 1942–1992.

In late 1943 Ed was finally transferred out of Tulagi of the Solomon islands for duty at Treasure Island in San Francisco Bay. He married the beautiful Mary Rae McArthur, the Beauty Queen of UCLA, and soon they had two sons, Tom and Steve. When the war was over, he returned to Santa Monica and finished a BA Degree at UCLA on the GI Bill.

A friend in the building business offered Ed the opportunity to go into business with him. Ed claimed he could have become a millionaire if he had accepted his friend's offer. But Ed claimed "I had sand in my toes." So Ed moved out to Honolulu and built condominiums and houses. He had learned construction trade from his father. At Honolulu he could still do his surfing and swimming and get "sand in his toes."

From his "Dreamer Fearon" days at Tulagi he hadn't forgotten his dream of Tahiti. In the early 1950's he went down to Tahiti with the idea of living there and possibly building some hotels. At Falls Church, Virginia where we lived, Ed visited while enroute to Paris to visit French banks for building hotel Bora Bora on that island and the Tahara on Tahiti. A Mr. Long, who owned the Long chain of drugstores of Oakland, California, offered to put up $250,000 on a gamble of having Ed build the two hotels. Ed got the loan from the French banks and he built the two beautiful world famous hotels.

Ed was divorced, and his two sons married Polynesian women and chose to live in Tahiti. Ed has always wanted to have a daughter so adopted a very young girl, Maoata, from a family of the Austral islands to the south of the Society Islands. He needed a woman to take care of his adopted daughter, and found Nieves from Lima, Peru, who became his housekeeper and friend. Nieves was very intelligent so Ed had her manage the boutique shop at Hotel Tahara for a number of years. Nieves became a French citizen of Tahiti.

Ed was director of the two hotels for a number of years. Eventually as part owner of the hotels, he retired and settled into his lovely home in Tahiti close to the Hotel Tahara. In 1976 Ed had invited my wife and I to visit him at Bora Bora where he had a house above the Bora

Bora Hotel. It was then that as an anthropologist, I became interested in making a study what happened to all the children sired by American GI's stationed on the island during WW II. Because of Ed's great hospitality, I returned to Tahiti many times to continue my study about the American and half Tahitian children.

I became good friends with many of these children who are now already grandparents.

Ed and Nieves live at Ed's beautiful home at Mahina of Tahiti during the cooler winter months, and they go to Auckland, New Zealand during hot Tahitian summer months. Also he visits his sister living in Sacramento, California. On these visits he now continues up to our home at Klamath Falls, Oregon. Luckily Ed, Bill Rom, and I—old WW II buddies—are still alive and keep up our correspondence and friendship over all these years since the war was finished in 1945.

BILL ROM

Born on December 5, 1917, Bill was left fatherless 30 days later when his dad was killed by a cave-in at the Chandler iron ore mine in Ely, Minnesota. Bills mother, with 8 children, thereafter made ends meet by taking in a boarder, cooking for Ely weddings which were a 3-day affair, raising a large garden, pigs and chickens.

Bill went on through school, graduation from the University of Minnesota in 1940 with a bachelor's degree in Wildlife Management, a new field at that time. He survived the great depression by peddling Sunday papers to the various Civilian Conservation Camps surrounding Ely in the Superior National Forest. Saving his money from peddling 400 papers which he paid 2 cent each for and sold for 10 cents, he purchased a 1925 Overland sedan for $65.00, which he used to commute to the camps, making up to $32.00 each Sunday.

A protégé of nationally known environmentalist Sigurd Olson, dean of the Ely Junior College, Sig was instrumental in obtaining summer jobs for Bill such as working on U.S. Forest Service trail crews and manning a remote fire tower in the Superior National Forest Boundary Waters Canoe Country Wilderness. Money from these jobs helped the cost of attending the University. With WW II impending in 1940, instead of following his field in wildlife management, Bill volunteered for the U.S. Navy. With three months open before being called to active duty, Bill hitchhiked out West to work in the mines to make ends meet. Relatives in Butte, Montana directed him to Burke, Idaho where they were hiring at the time. Robert Ripley's "Believe it or Not" column had at one time listed Burke as being the narrowest town in the country, where the railroad tracks went up the main and only street, necessitating the cutting out of a section of the town's large boarding house to let the train through. Bill first took a job on a Union Pacific Railroad track crew as a ghandi dancer, which is about the toughest job one can have, paying $4.65 per day. Thirty five cents per day was taken out from this sum for a retirement account. Shortly thereafter Bill was hired by the

Custer Consolidated Mining Co. to work in a lead and zinc mine under Custer Peak as timberman's helper. This job paid $5.00 per day. His partner had been born in Winton, Minnesota, only 5 miles from Bills home town of Ely, Mn. After several months on this job Bill went back to Butte where they commenced hiring, to be with his relatives, two of his mother's sisters and their families. He first worked in the Mt. Con Copper Mine, 4,400 feet down as miner's helper, and then as a motorman in the Tramway mine where it was drier and safer to work.

Epilogue 145

"Wild" Bill Rom's Dream Woman of
Figi -1942

Young Navy Communication officers
of Tulagi with a souviner from a
battle field on Guadalcanal.

Lt Commander Bill Rom

A delay caused by Navy orders being lost in the mail which would have taken him to Guantanamo, Cuba on a training cruise, gave him nine months to work on these various jobs, until being called to active duty on June, 1941. Bill had to forgo a job as a sightseeing bus driver in Yellowstone National Park which would have taken him out of the mines, to report for active duty in the Navy. First duty was to attend the midshipman's school at Northwestern University at Chicago, where he first met the Great Swede Tom Larson, overhearing him talking about Sig Olson.

Next duty was in Naval Intelligence in Seattle where Bill met Barb, a lovely University of Washington coed. It was love at first sight and an eventual 58 years of marriage with four children and seven grandchildren. Marriage took place in 1944 at Grace Cathedral in San Francisco during a short leave from duty, with friend Tom as best man.

Naval service included a year on the battlewagon U.S.S. Maryland, a year on Guadalcanal and Tulagi, where we meet Tom again, a short period on the carrier U.S.S. Bismark Sea, which was blasted in two at Iwo Jima just after getting transferred off the ship, thankfully. A kamikaze had flown into the hangar deck, setting off the stored torpedoes and bombs, resulting in loss of half the crew. I was the first lieutenant on the ship with a battle station on the very bottom.

Next was duty on the attack transport U.S.S. Navarro as first lieutenant and cargo officer, with interim deck duty conning the ship. We made the initial landing on Okinawa on April 1, 1945 where it took us six days to unload the cargo. We also carried several hundred troops aboard. We made the fleet record for unloading our 32 landing craft and troops during the landing.

Of our four children our oldest son Bill Jr., is director of pulmonary medicine at Bellevue Hospital in New York City, and is also on the medical research staff at NYU. He has a Masters in public health as well as an M.D. He actually saw the twin towers collapse during 9–11. He and his lovely artistic wife Holly have two girls. Nicole has just returned from six months in Tanzania, while attending Bates College, and two years in the Peace Corps in Kazakhstan. She currently is enrolled in the master's program of environmental studies at the University of Michigan. Meredith is an honor student at Rye Senior High School.

Our daughter Becky is a law partner with Faegre and Benson in Minneapolis, the second largest law firm in the city. She's a former aerobatic pilot and guided for her dad's canoe trip outfitting company. She is very active in wilderness preservation and currently is chairperson of the governing council of the Wilderness Society, a 1.4 million member association. Becky is married to an attorney and has two boys, one in high school and the other attending Colorado State University.

Our second son Larry is an accomplished bush pilot who flew for three firms in Alaska and currently is operating our fly-in outpost camp in Ontario, Canada. He is still single but has a steady girl friend here in Ely.

Son Roger is an assistant district attorney in Anchorage, Alaska, married to Marcia who is also an attorney, and they have three lovely daughters fourteen and under.

After the war Bill and Barb started Canoe Country Outfitters, Inc. in Ely, Minnesota, which eventually became the largest outfitting company in America. We serviced parties going into the Quetico-Superior wilderness by canoe. Bill had taken over 50 canoe trips in his life time and Barb has taken numerous trips as well.

Barb and Bill retired in 1975 after 30 years in the outfitting business. Time now is spent traveling throughout the world mostly in the winter, and gardening during the summer months. Bill has given up hunting after a lifetime of trips through Ontario, including shooting 81 deer and 16 moose, as well as countless ducks and geese, grouse and ptarmigan. Live and let live is his policy now, as well as living by the golden rule. He currently is being urged by the Great Swede to write up his autobiography, which is a task of the future.

Epilogue for Thomas J. Larson

On April 10th, 1917, 1 was born on a farm near Kerkoven in western Minnesota. This event occurred four days after America declared WAR on Germany April 6th. When I was about two years old, my father Elmer became a county agent at Mora, Minnesota. He was a full-blooded Swede. His father, the oldest of ten brothers and sisters with their parents, immigrated from southern Sweden in 1869 to America. They settled on homestead land near Murdock, Minnesota. For five miles their farms were along a road which became known as Larson Road.

My mother, Myrna Pressnell, was from Duluth, Minnesota. Her father, Captain Thomas H. Pressnell was a Civil War veteran of the famous lst Minnesota regiment in the Army of the Potomac. As an infant he was brought from Shipton, Underwychwood, Oxfordshire, England to America. He was never to know England. My mother's people were Parkers and Quakers from Philadelphia. Her grandfather Edward Parker sailed around the world on Old Ironsides as a sailor. Later he moved to Duluth, Minnesota where he became a teacher and a judge.

At Mora, Minnesota my sisters Virginia, Marjorie, and Barbara were born. My distinguished mother had graduated from the University of Minnesota in 1914, There she was vice president of her senior class, on the debate team, Mortar Board, extemporaneous speaker, and in the Delta Gamma society. Her first employment upon graduation was to teach English at the farm-boys' Extension Division at Crookston, Minnesota, where my father was a student. They fell in love and were married in 1915.

In 1922 my father accepted a position to be in charge of WW I veterans at a logging settlement called Veteransville in Aitkin County. There my youngest sister Patricia was born. There was no school in this wild primitive settlement thus in 1923 the family was moved to the small town of Aitkin along the Mississippi River. I went all through school in this delightful small town surrounded by beautiful forests and many lakes. At age 12 I joined the Boy Scouts, and by fourteen had earned the rank of Eagle. I had a wonderful life of roaming the forest and lake country. As my parents had the Puritan ethic of hard work during the depression years, I had my first job at age nine making berry boxes at forty five cents a day for several weeks during summer vacation. I had a wide variety of boyhood jobs, and learned to save whatever I could for attending the University of Minnesota. In Aitkin High School I was class president two years, a member of the football team three years, and Captain of the track team in my senior year. I won my events of high hurdles, and discus, and went to the State meet in Minneapolis in 1935.

Also while I was in high school, I was a member of Company B of the 135 Minnesota National Guard Regiment which was a descendant of the famous First Minnesota Regiment of the Civil War. But I was destined to join the Navy for World War Two.

After attending two years at the University of Minnesota where I studied liberal arts—mostly biological sciences then forestry—I embarked on a scout vagabond journey around the world. With a pack on my back I hitch-hiked to Seattle, then down to San Pedro, California. There I luckily became a sailor for four months on a coastwise oil tanker the winter of 1938. I saved my salary and hitch-hiked and rode on top of freight trains to New York City.

My good luck continued, and I was able to get the opportunity to work my passage in August on an Isbrandtsen-Moller freighter to Antwerp, Belgium. Upon arrival there I bought a new bicycle for twenty dollars and set out for high adventure. I cycled through Holland. then took passage to England, thence to Wales, over to Ireland, and back to Scotland and down to Newcastle, England. From there I sailed to Bergen, Norway, then cycled to Denmark, Sweden, Finland, over to Estonia, Latvia, Lithuania, Poland and into Nazi Germany. I could see how Germany was preparing for war.

Cycling on to Paris, France, I met my great friend, fellow Eagle Scout Edwin Woolverton, at the Youth Hostel. He too had worked passage on an Isbrandtsen-Moller freighter out of New York. We cycled down to Marseilles, then took a four dollar deck passage to Bone, Algeria.

Our cycle journey now took us to Tunis of Tunesia, and we settled in at a youth hostel at fascinating Sidi Bou Said overlooking the Bay of Tunis.

Not being able to get a passage on a British ship for Australia where we planned to attend the International scout jamboree, we ended up in January of 1939 headed for Italy. We hitch-hiked up to Rome from the seaport Civitavecchia. From a hostel we ventured out into fascinating

Rome where we saw Fascist legions marching also in preparation for the coming World War Two.

We took a cheap train trip up into northern Italy, and crossed Lake Como into Switzerland. From there it was to Freiberg, Germany, across the Rhine River to Colmar France and thence back to Paris. There we settled in once again, and made numerous side trip around France. Up at Antwerp, Belgium we tried to get a ship that would take us further to the east and around the world. Having no luck, we hitch-hiked up to Holland and into western Germany, then back to Antwerp.

Luckily we got a promised job back with an Isbrandtsen-Moller freighter in April just four months before the Nazis invaded Poland. We crossed the north Atlantic in a huge storm with an 18 day crossing to New York. My journey in Europe, Britain and north Africa cost me $240 for ten months and with about $2,000 worth of Boy Scout hospitality.

In 1940 I was back at the University of Minnesota. But I'd smelled the fragrant eucalyptus trees on the University of California Berkeley campus. It was bye bye Minnesota. Once again I shouldered my pack sack and hitch-hiked to Berkeley. Luckily I was admitted to the spring semester of 1941 at this great university. In June I hitch-hiked back to my home in Minnesota. I'd taken a midshipman cruise out of New York the summer of 1940, and now I was headed for Northwestern University in Chicago for my three month Naval Reserve training. There I had the great good fortune to meet Bill Rom. I became a Reserve Ensign, and on December 7th, 1941, I was delivering messages to Admiral Kimmil and his CinCPac Staff at the Battle of Pearl Harbor.

Hurrah! As soon as World War Two was over I had enough points to get out of the Navy and pursue my ambition of becoming a scientist and explorer. From the USS Lexington aircraft carrier, I left this mighty ship at Eniwetok atoll and transferred as a passenger to the Jeep carrier Manila Bay on October 6th, 1945. We were headed for San Francisco, and arrived there on October 19th, 1945. There I was processed out—a most glorious day—on October 23rd, 1945. My first wife, Dorothy Ratcliff, and I hitch-hiked to our original home to Aitkin, Minnesota. I planned a learning-how-to-be-an-explorer expedition to Peten Province of northern Guatemala. I would collect mammal and reptile study specimens for the American Museum of Natural History of New York, and also explore for Maya ruins.

Before heading south down along the Mississippi River to New Orleans, we celebrated Christmas at Aitkin, and had a holiday with old friend Ed Woolverton at his island cabin on Lake Vermillion in northern Minnesota. Ed had joined me at Paris while I was on a Boy Scout vagabond journey by bicycle then later by hitchhiking. That story will appear in my book THE VAGABONDS ESCAPE FROM EUROPE IN 1939 to be published in 2003.

Dorothy and I drove down along the great river in a second-hand pickup van all the way to New Orleans stopping in Missouri to visit Comdr. Bill Coultas I'd met out in the Solomons. He taught me how to prepare mammal specimens for museums, and listed equipment we would need before we got to Guatemala.

In New Orleans no cargo ships had been released from the Navy, and especially one sailing to Belize, British Honduras. We lived at a tourist camp and spent about a month collecting expedition supplies. Also I made trips to Tulane University to study about the Maya at their Middle America Institute. Finally in mid January we got a cargo ship that took us to the seaport of Belize. From there we rode mules with our equipment up to the Guatemala border. From there we were flown on an old tri-motored Ford plane to Flores, Peten.

Our headquarters was on Flores Island. From there we spent six months exploring at Uaxactun, to Tikal, and La Libertad. I made a special trip to Piedras Negras on the Ursamacinta River on the border of Mexico where I filmed a small family of the Lacondone Indians. I had this expedition in an article I had published in the December 1969 edition of the Explorers Journal.

In August of 1946 we returned to Aitkin, Minnesota briefly, then went to Richmond, California to find a cheap place to live. I registered at the University of California at Berkeley on the G.I. Bill. In June of 1947 1 had earned a BA Degree in anthropology. Luckily I now became a member of Wendell Phillip's University of California Africa Expedition. Professor Charles Camp of the UC Paleontology Department would head this southern branch of the expedition while Wendell would lead the northern group. My job was to collect mammal and reptile specimens as study specimens for the Museum of Vertebrate Zoology there at Berkeley. I kept a journal, and am perhaps the only survivor of the southern branch of this epic expedition. My travels and collecting took me from Port Elizabeth, to Cape Town, up to Windhoek, to Ovamboland and the Kaokaveld of South West Africa. Then back to the Cape I traveled and up into the Transvaal to join Professor Camp and Dr. Frank Peabody at Gladysvale Farm. I plan to publish my story in a book I will name THE GREAT ADVENTURE (The University of California South Africa Expedition of 1947–1948). I collected specimens also at Krueger Park and over into Mozambique.

I'd fallen love with Africa so did not return back to Berkeley with the other members of the expedition. I took a job on a geophysical survey for the Roan Antelope Copper Company for four months at Luynshya, of Northern Rhodesia. I made a Christmas Holiday trip up to Elizabethville of the Belgian Congo. I've written an unpublished novel about this adventure. From there in 1949 I returned to Cape Town and became a G.I. student in anthropology and archaeology at the University of Cape Town.

My anthropology Professor Issac Schapera now sent me up to Namaqualand for some fieldwork experience recording the folk tales of the Cape Coloured Hottentots at Liliefontein Reserve. Then he got permission from the Bechuanaland Protectorate authorities for me to do fieldwork up on the BaKwena Reserve at Molepolole to study ethno-zoology. While there I collected mammal and reptile study specimens for the American Museum of Natural History of New York. In August of 1950 I went up to Ngamiland at Maun, then around the Okavango Delta up to Shakawe along the Okavango River where I began my study of the culture of the Hambukushu. This beginning research I was able to use for a MA Degree in anthropology at American University in Washington D.C., and a MLitt at the University of Oxford in 1968.

The period from 1949 to 1956 is recorded in my published book entitled : BLIKSEM TRAVELS WITH A SOUTH AFRICAN DOG published in 2001 Then in early 1951 Bliksem and I sailed up to England, then over to Holland and thence to Germany. I became employed by the Cultural Branch of the American State Department to present my Bushman-Hambukushu movie to German audiences at the Amerika Houses in Western Germany. In December of 1951, we—the dog and I—went to Berkeley, California, where I lectured for the University of California Extension Division, and took other jobs. Then-hurrah! In 1953 we met Miss Carolyn Collier and the faithful hound and I pursued Carolyn in cold December to Hamburg, Germany, where she was employed by the International Refugee Organization to help eastern European refugees find homes abroad.

We were married by the Standesampt in Hamburg. Then hurrah! I most fortunately got a job with the U.S. Airforce as an educational advisor for the 66th Tactical Recon Wing. We had another wedding for the Air Force at Weisbaden, and finally a church wedding in Geneva, Switzerland. It was three weddings and eventually three children. Baby Laurel was born September 16th, 1954, at Landstuhl U.S. Army hospital. In 1956 we returned to America and moved to Prince Georges County adjacent to Washington D.C. I became employed with the Human Relations Area File at the American University doing research on a book for the US Army on Saudi Arabia. Carolyn became a social worker at the D.C. Hospital.

After a year of African Studies at Boston University (1956–1957), in 1959, I became an education advisor for Dover Air Force Base in Delaware until 1960. I would drive home to Falls Church, Virginia on weekends and back to the air base at Dover early mornings on Monday—120 miles one way. Our son Tom was born at Arlington Hospital, Virginia on February 24th, 1959. Carolyn had a social work job in Falls Church.

In 1960 I had a position with International Education at the U.S. Office of Education in Washington D. C. as a program officer for foreign graduate students sponsored by the State Department. I finally finished my MA Degree at American University in anthropology in early 1962 then joined USAID, and our little family was flown to Addis Ababa of Ethiopia. I had a position in the Education Division and got to travel far and wide throughout Ethiopia. Our youngest daughter Janet was born in a hospital behind the Emporer's palace on May 16th, 1962.

After a three weeks' holiday out in the Seychelles Islands, I had a lucky mid-tour transfer to Lome, Togo of West Africa. I worked in community development north of Lama-Kara developing an agricultural school to train county agents. In 1964 we returned to Falls Church, Virginia and I was reemployed by US Office of Education. For two terms I taught anthropology in 1966 at the University of Maryland at College Park campus. Then in late August of that year we sailed to England where I became a M Litt graduate student in social anthropology at the University of Oxford. We lived at nearby Woodstock. Carolyn had a job as a socialworker at Radcliffe Hospital in Oxford, and I taught for the University of Maryland Overseas program at American air bases.

Upon finishing my M Litt studies we moved to Johannesburg, South Africa where I taught for two years at the University of the Witwatersrand. During university holidays I carried out anthropological field studies of the Hambukushu African tribe who lived along the Okavango River of Ngamiland, Botswana. Carolyn had a social work position at the Tara Hospital in Johannesburg. We returned to our home at Falls Church, Virginia. I became employed to teach anthropology and sociology at the Northern Virginia Community College until 1983. During this time I also taught anthropology in evenings for the University College of the University of Maryland, and the Extension Division for the University of Virginia as an adjunct professor. During this time I completed a PhD Degree in anthropology at the University of Virginia. Also during that time I organized and led 30 college credit field trips abroad for my students. Also during this time Carolyn was employed as a social worker at Fairfax Hospital.

In 1983 we moved to Klamath Falls, Oregon. Our three children all completed university studies. Laurel did a BA and MA at George Washington University. Tom did a BA Degree at Seattle University and his MA at California

State University at Chico, California. Janet did a BA at the University of Virginia, and a MBA at Harvard. I returned several times with grants from the National Geographic Society for research with the Kabiye tribe of Togo in 1985, then another grant in 1987–88 to study the Bayeyi and Hambukushu of Ngamiland, Botswana. Again in 1994 I returned to the Hambukushu along the Okavango River to study social change.

During our residence in Pine Grove of Klamath Falls, I made numerous journeys to Tahiti and Bora Bora of the Society Islands to study what happened to the children left behind on Bora Bora with American G.I. fathers stationed there in World War II. Also I returned to Virginia several times to teach at Northern Virginia Community college. I also taught at the Oregon Institute of Technology at Klamath Falls and Klamath Community College where I still teach at age 85. Over the years I wrote many books (manuscripts) which I had bound. Now I am having them published by the Writers Club Press of Lincoln, Nebraska.

0-595-27756-X